Postcards From Paradise

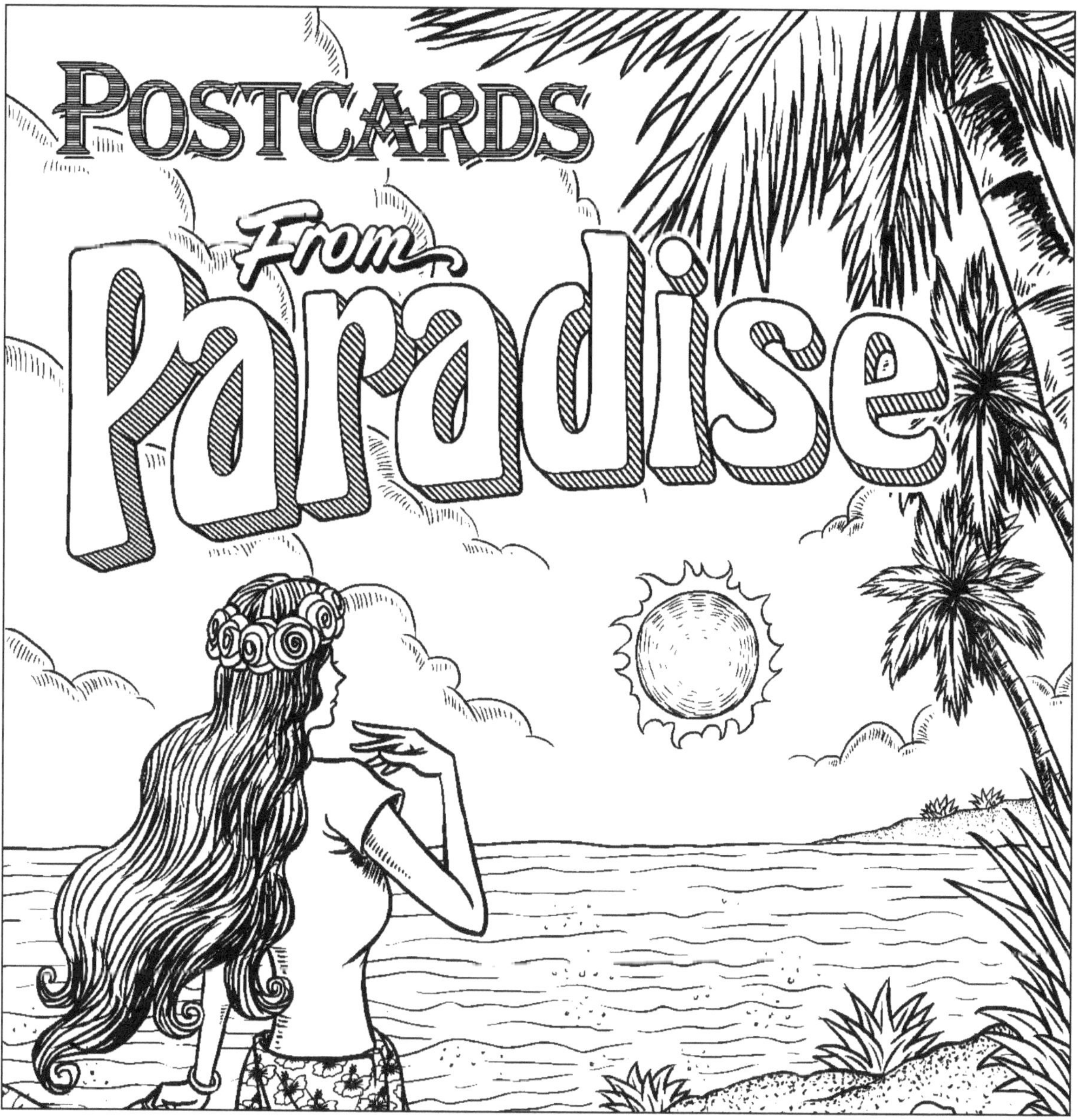

A Tropical Coloring & Activity Book

By Connie Gorrell

ISBN-10:0-9982651-2-8
ISBN-13:978-0-9982651-2-4

www.Inspirations.International

Printed in the U.S.A.

Inspirations International

Creative Works to Inspire the World

The waves echo behind me. Patience–Faith–Openness, is what the sea has to teach. Simplicity–Solitude–Intermittency...
But there are other beaches to explore.
There are more shells to find.
This is only a beginning.

Annie Morrow Lindbergh
A Gift From the Sea

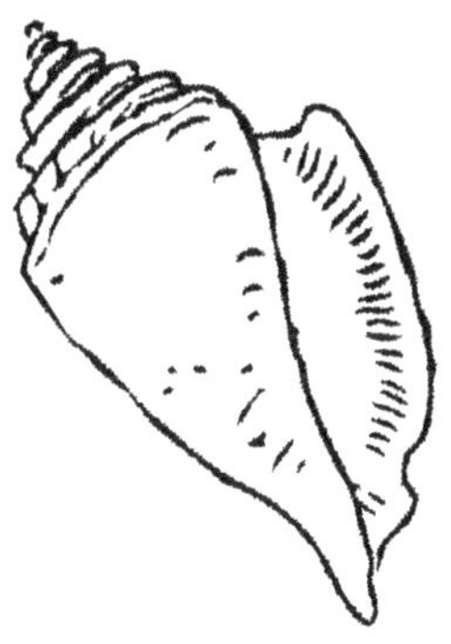

Welcome to Postcards From Paradise!

Are you going on vacation? *Take me, take me*!

Postcards From Paradise is not an average coloring book for adults. It's your perfect holiday vacation companion book!

You won't find a blitz of blinding dots and squiggles as seen in traditional adult coloring books. Those pages are monotonous and they take forever to complete. One fellow we know took well over a year to complete *one* coloring page! Of course, he did not color every day but each time he did he felt he made very little progress. He did, however, reap the meditative and relaxing benefits of coloring.

Postcards From Paradise presents you with quick tropical themed coloring pages that can be completed and admired in a sitting or two and at your own pace. It includes activities such as a variety of fun puzzles and journal pages, called **SUNBEAMS** for your enjoyment and reflection.

Your Personal Color Pallet: NATURE

The love of nature resonates deep within our very essence. It makes us feel alive and connects us to something mysterious and powerful. As you step inside these pages and begin to transcend into the tropical scenes, you will mimic nature's own display of color and light while sensing and feeling its energy. Nature is our inspiration. It is the ultimate *master artist* that endows us with breathtaking vistas and perfect pallets of spectral light that surrounds every aspect of our lives. In a word: COLOR!

Creating Color

When electromagnetic waves of light hit an object some of the waveforms are absorbed while others are reflected. These effects are what our brain visually interprets as **COLOR**.

- When all of the waveforms are *absorbed*, we see black.
- When all of the waveforms are *reflected*, we see white.
- When *some* of the wavelengths are absorbed and *some* are reflected we see colors

Nature enriches and enhances colors, even monochromes (one color). For example, the ocean may be monochromatic (blue) but look closely. How does the interplay of light and shadow turn the hues of blues into brilliant shades of the same color? Keep this in mind as you color the scenes and create your own private paradise.

Color Your World

When you begin to engage in the soothing tropical scenes in ***Postcards From Paradise*** take notice of what attracts you. What are your favorite colors and what do they say about you? Are you attracted to warm tones, or do cooler colors catch your eye?

Yellows, reds and oranges are considered warm colors. They appear to move forward, appearing closer to your eye. Blues, greens and purples are considered cool colors. These colors appear to move further away from the eye. You can harmonize these colors in every scene of this book. Think of the contrasts: lush palm trees fringing the bright sandy shores of an azure blue ocean at sunset, or the brilliant array of tropical flowers shining in the golden sunlight.

BONUS Section: To learn how to infuse meditation with chroma (color) therapy, read on. Otherwise, skip ahead to the "Ready, Set, Color!" section and the coloring & activity pages that are waiting to cast your sails into the wind and whisk you away.

How to Use Chromatherapy for Relaxation & Meditation

Color is electromagnetic energy. Did you know that *everything* is energy? Quantum physics (Ack! *Physics*? It's okay—just this one point, I promise) shows us that everything in our universe is energy. Energy is vibration and each vibration has a frequency. The same goes with color. Each color has a vibration all its own and evokes a physical response associated with it. In this section, you will learn how to link specific vibratory colors to your body's energetic channels. They are called your ***chakras***.

Chakra is the Sanskrit word for *wheel*, such as the color wheel on the back cover. The color wheel is divided into seven sections and each one represents an energy center of your body. These energy centers, called chakras, are aligned from the base of your spine to the top of your head. Each one has a unique symbolic color vibration associated with it.

I love how everything in natures is intertwined. Each of our body's energy channels (chakras) relate to an element of nature. As you add your unique flair to these pages, focus on each color vibration. Relate them to the elements: earth, air, fire, water, and spirit. Breathe in a bit of balance for your mind and body by allowing yourself to escape into paradise, if only for a while. This is your time for reflection, meditation, prayer—your personal connection to Nature.

Below, I have listed the basics of the chakras, where they are located, and their corresponding colors. There is an affirmation associated with each one. Reflect and relax as you color. This is the greatest therapy ever, and it costs practically nothing! As you focus or meditate on each color, or chakra, envision that specific area of your body. Infuse it with its symbolic color as you revel in the tropical scenes. Write about your experiences in the journal pages, or jot down anything you wish. This is *your* world! Are you ready? It's time to feel light, feel free, and have some fun!

The Chakras and Their Energetic Colors

Reflect on each color and its symbolism as your creative flow designs each tropical scene as only *you* can. Focus on the affirmation for each one as you color your scenes.

First chakra:

ROOT. It sits at the base of your spine. Represents relation to Earth; survival instincts

Red: *I am strong, grounded, stable and ignited.*

- Red is associated with primal urges, messages of passion and power
- The most dense of all colors and implies physical movement and vitality
- Illuminates sunsets and emblazes tropical flowers with passionate crimson reds

Second chakra:

SACRAL. It sits in the area of your naval. Reproduction, joy, compassion

Orange: *I am creative and open to new experiences.*

- Orange is associated with creativity, feelings, sociability, exploration and endurance
- Blended between red (aggression) and yellow (optimism) orange suggests harmony
- Is the color of citrus, sunrise and sunset

Third chakra:

SOLAR PLEXUS. It is located in the area just below your breastbone; the center of our being and the seat of personal power and awareness

Yellow: ***I am content, centered and empowered.***

- Yellow represents joy, optimism, happiness, imagination, intuition, enthusiasm and hope
- Is the brightest color the human eye is able to see. The color of sunshine and summer
- Inner vison that evokes pleasant and cheerful feelings, radiates creativity and intellect

Fourth chakra:

HEART. It is located in the center of your chest; center of Love

Green: ***Within me lies the eternal love of nature.***

- Green represents growth, nature, health and luck; has balancing and healing powers
- Lush color of land, trees, and grasses signifying growth and acceptance
- Signifies stability, safety and endurance; also wealth and money

Fifth chakra:

THROAT. It is located at the base of your larynx; center of communication

Blue: ***I communicate openly with love and peace.***

- Blue represents the color of sea and sky; soothes the spirit and soul
- Symbolizes expression, intelligence, trust, loyalty, wisdom, faith, truth
- Soothing to the eye and associated with healing, tranquility, sincerity, and calmness

Sixth chakra:

'THIRD EYE.' It is located in the middle of your forehead and represents wisdom, intuition, deeper understanding and spiritual awareness

Indigo: ***I look deeper to my intuition and awareness with wisdom.***

- Indigo runs deep in color like the unknown depths of the ocean; always present, inviting us to dive in and discover energy patterns and rhythms
- Signifies emotion, strength, fluidity, perception, and expression, sixth sense
- Is a color associated with night when our senses become more keen and intense

Seventh chakra:

CROWN. This sits at the top of your head like a crown. Connects us to the Divine, inner sense of wholeness and spiritual enlightenment

Violet: ***I surrender to the highest good with a sense of knowing and devotion.***

- Violet combines the stability of blue and the energy of red; the unifying color of oneness, spirituality, prestige, and royalty

- Displays fragile flowers and sleepy sunsets; like spring's first violet crocus opening its petals to the light of a new spring, peeling back layers of time and connection
- Signifies transformation and tranquility, the promise of something new, mystery and magic

What about the rest of the colors in your pack? They're important, too!

Shades of Pink:

- Universal color of romance and femininity; represents tenderness, compassion, and love
- The deeper the pink color, the more passion, playfulness and energy.
- Color of nature's most beautiful sea shells and florals; emblazes an evening sunset

Aqua and Turquoise Shades:

- Strengthens creativity, communication, and inspiration as deep as the sea
- Balances the mind and emotion; promotes spiritual development and happiness
- Strong and independent; symbolizes credibility

Browns:

- Down to earth color; symbolizes stability and structure
- Emphasizes a strong need for material security
- Practical and realistic. Represents earth, hearth, home

Gold:

- Exudes confidence, charm, and riches
- Spiritual energy and passion; rays of the sun
- Illumination, wisdom and wealth

Silver:

- Opens up new ideas and intuition
- Wealth and riches
- Moonlight on the water

Black and Gray:

- Is the result of complete absence, or absorption, of light
- Contains no shades in its purest form
- Power, elegance, and sophistication; mystery, grief

White:

- Contains no shades in their purest form because it is the combination of all colors
- Associated with light, goodness, purity, rebirth
- Coolness, cleanliness; depicts peace

Get Ready, Set, Color!

Call me old-fashioned, but I still love the feel of a crayon in my hand. I love how they smell and the memories they evoke—but that's just me. Stores today are full of colored pencil packs to suit the taste of every coloring book-loving connoisseur.

If you are on vacation, take time to relax…*really* relax. Do some deep breathing and let the stress of everyday life dissipate, then delve in. Your world in ***Postcards From Paradise*** awaits you. Become infused with the warmth of the sun, the sound of waves lapping on the shore, the aroma of tropical plumeria. Breathe deep and savor. Exhale, releasing all that which binds you to your pain or source of aggravation. Take a bug slurp of a fresh and fruity tropical drink and sink your toes into the warm sand.

If you are not on vacation ***Postcards From Paradise*** is waiting to take you far away to tropical islands where the trade winds blow gently through your hair, the sunshine embraces you, and lush, swaying palm trees beckon you to come. Sit. Relax. Enjoy. Breathe.

Lock the door. You are now on vacation.

Postcards From Paradise has something for everyone. If your mind has not slowed down yet, or you need some stimulation, try your hand at the puzzles and activities. These were designed especially for *you*! Relish the **SUNBEAM** journal pages. They are for your thoughts, dreams, doodles, lists, or memories.

Enjoy the journey!

Connie

There is nothing more miserable in the world than to arrive in paradise and look like your passport photo.

~Erma Bombeck

It's a toes-in-the-sand kind of day.
Go **Easy Barefootin'** down the path to find your center.

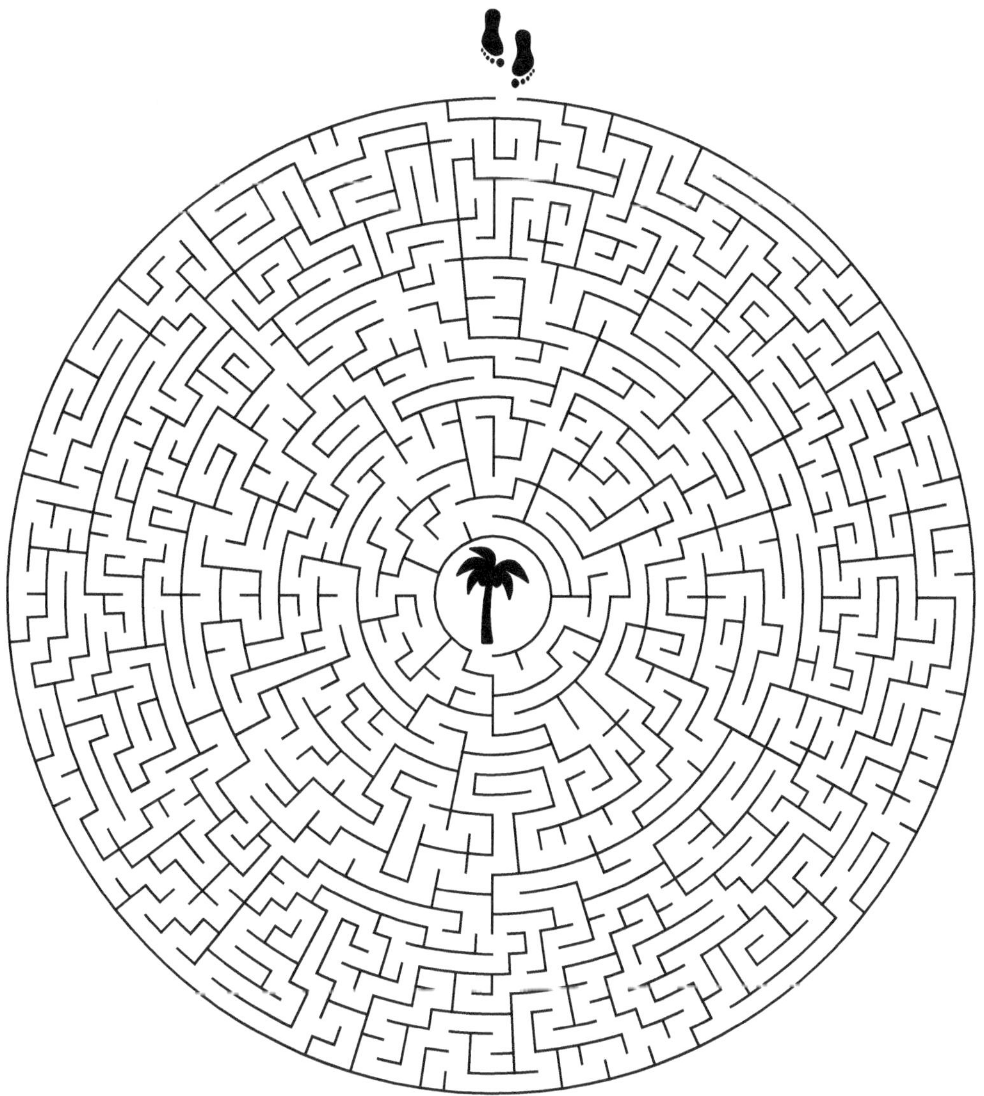

(*The solutions to all puzzles are in the back of the book.*)

Take the **Long Way Home** ~ Challenge Maze

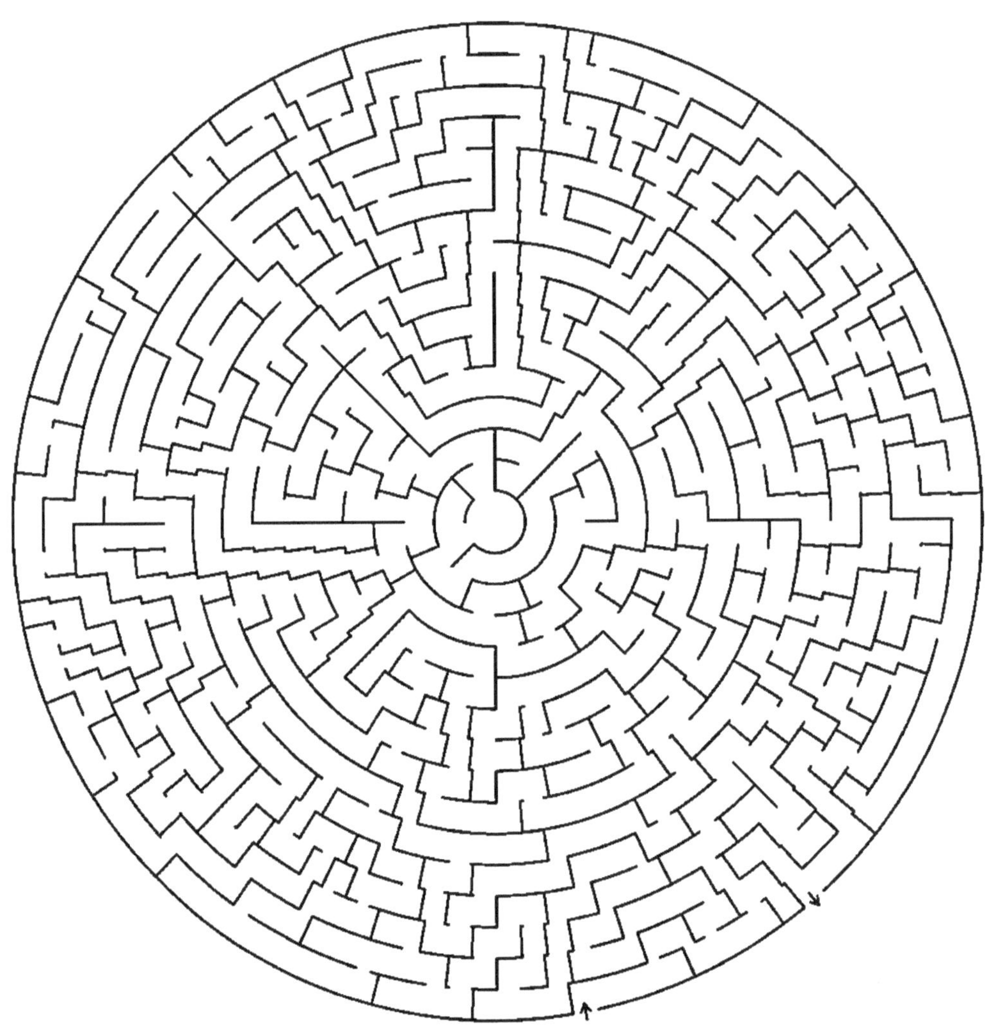

Start and finish here

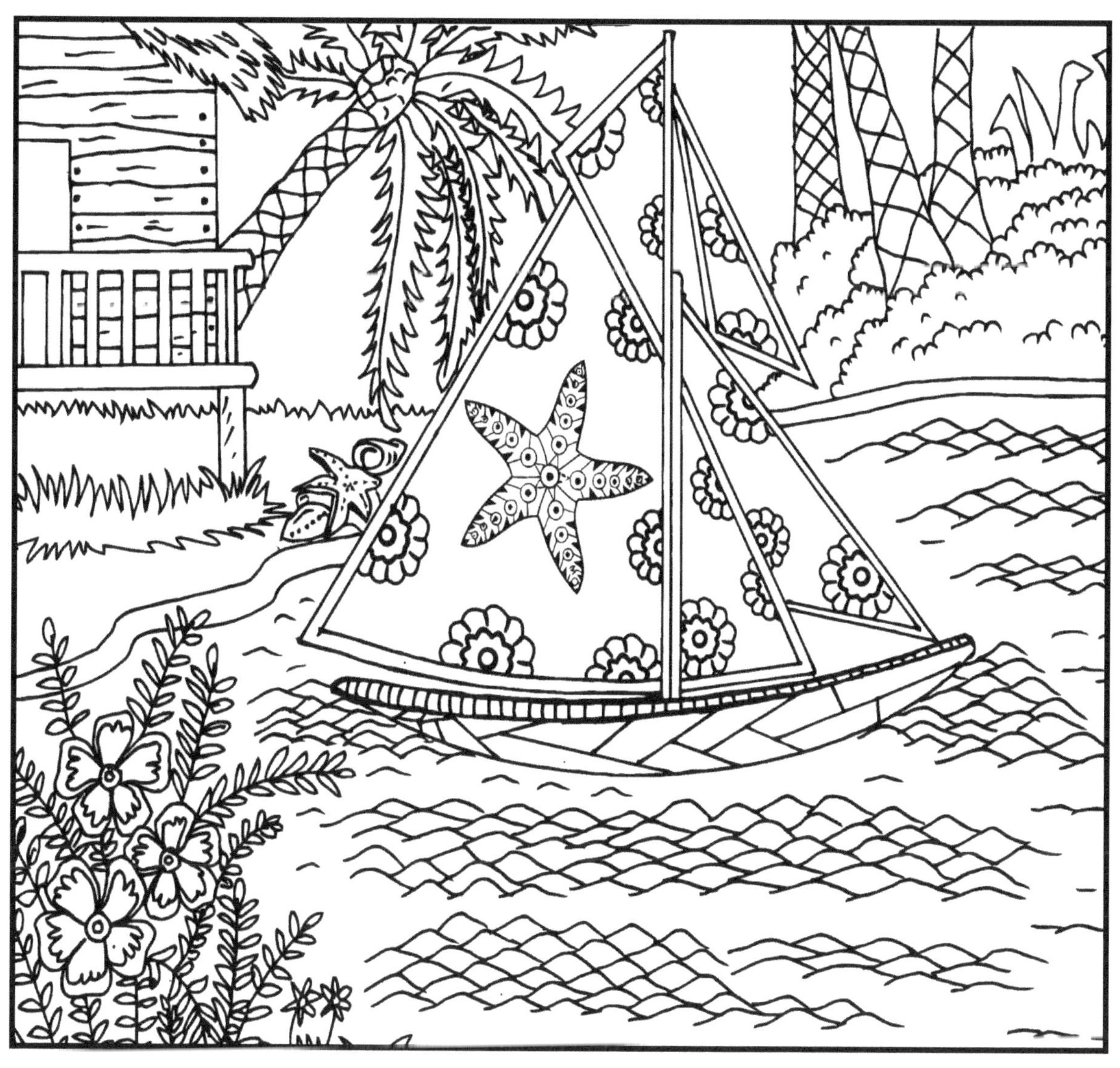

Someone asked me, if I were stranded on a desert island what book would I bring—"How to Build a Boat." ~Steven Wright

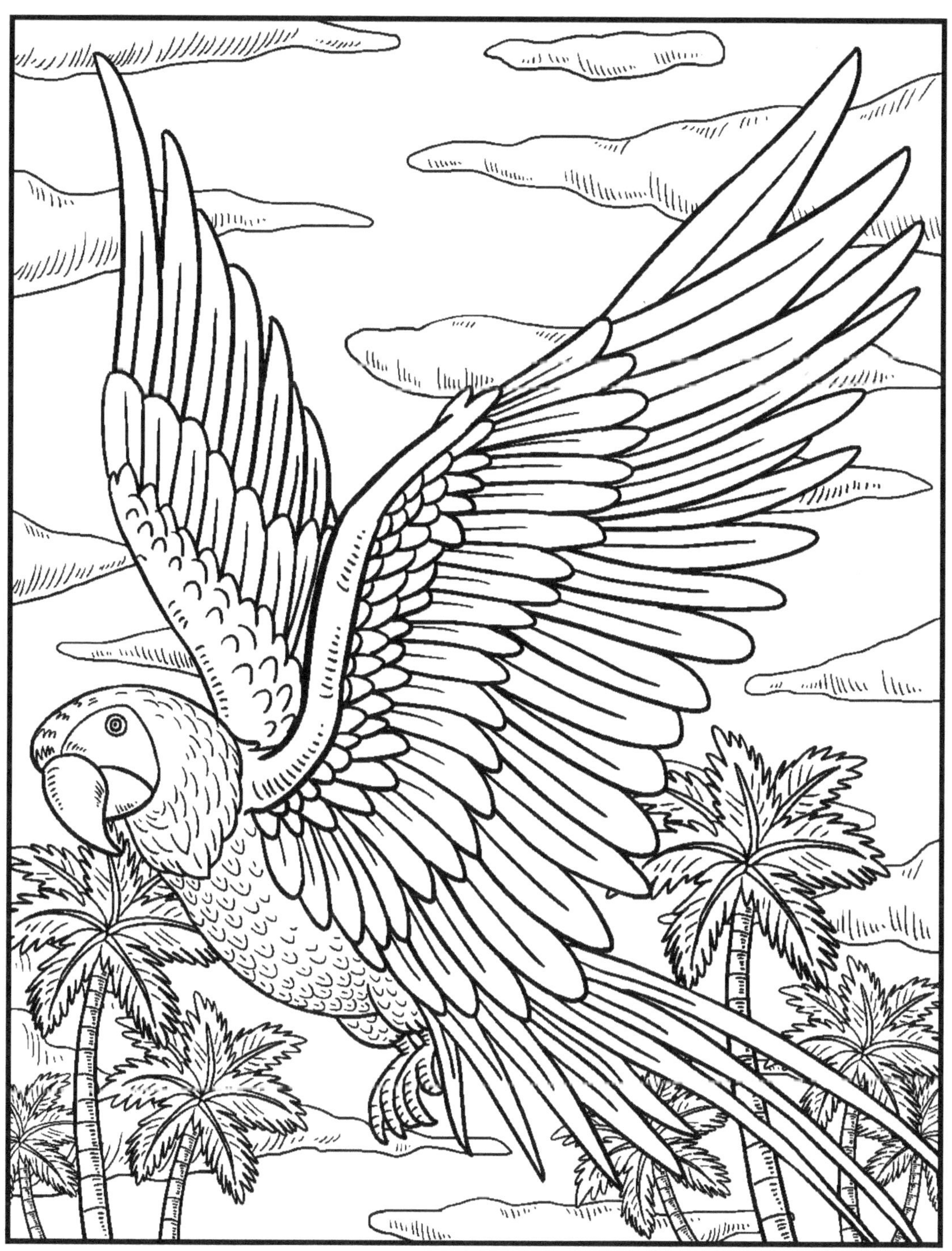

I spread my wings in glorious wonder & let my Spirit soar!

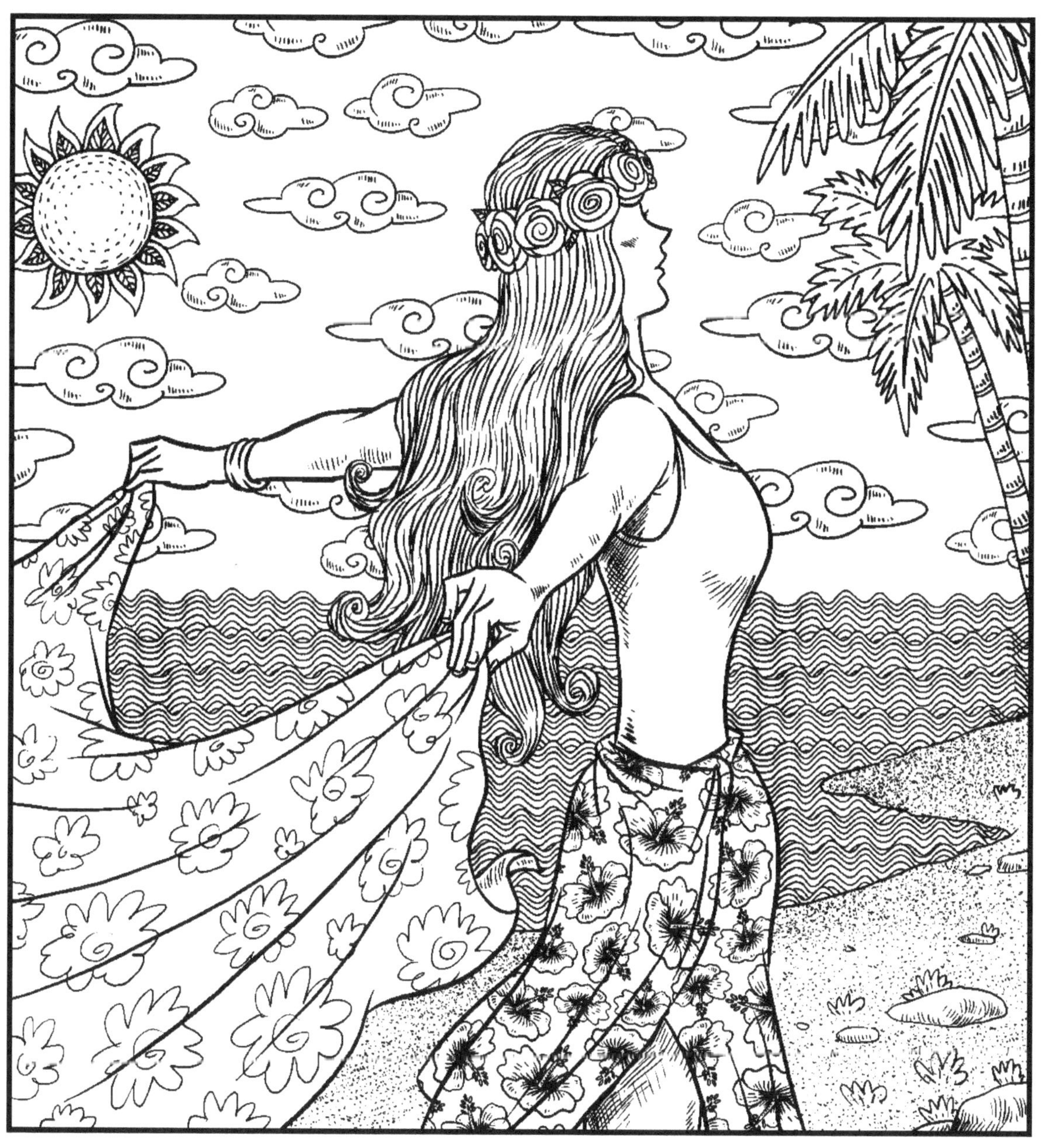

We travel, some of us forever, to seek other places, other lives, other souls.

~Anais Nin

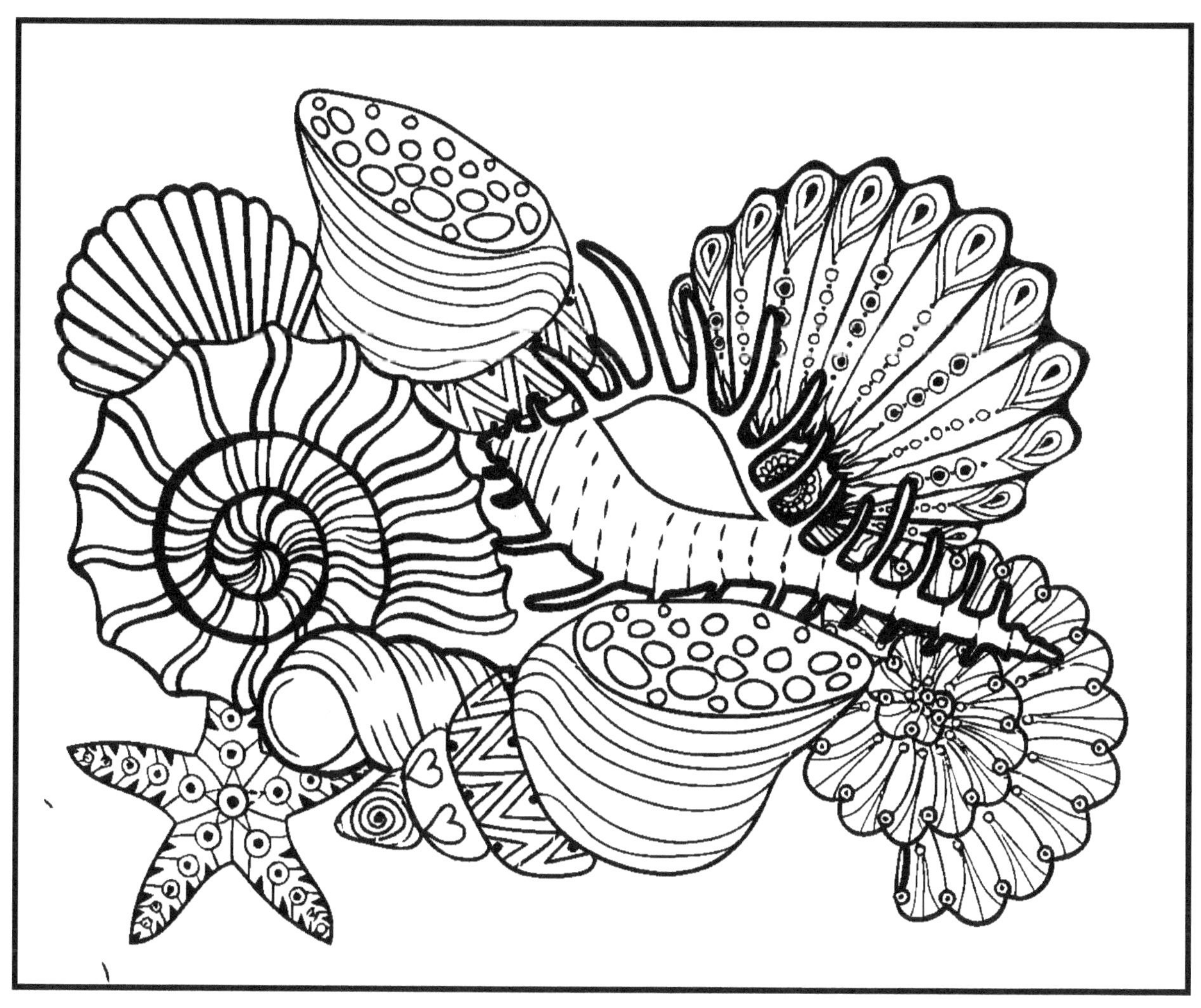

One cannot collect all the beautiful shells on the beach. One can only collect a few, and they are more beautiful if they are few. One moon shell is more impressive than three. There is only one moon in the sky... Gradually one discards and keeps just the perfect specimen; not necessarily a rare shell, but a perfect one of its kind. One sets it apart by itself, ringed around by space—like the island.

~Annie Morrow Lindbergh
A Gift From the Sea

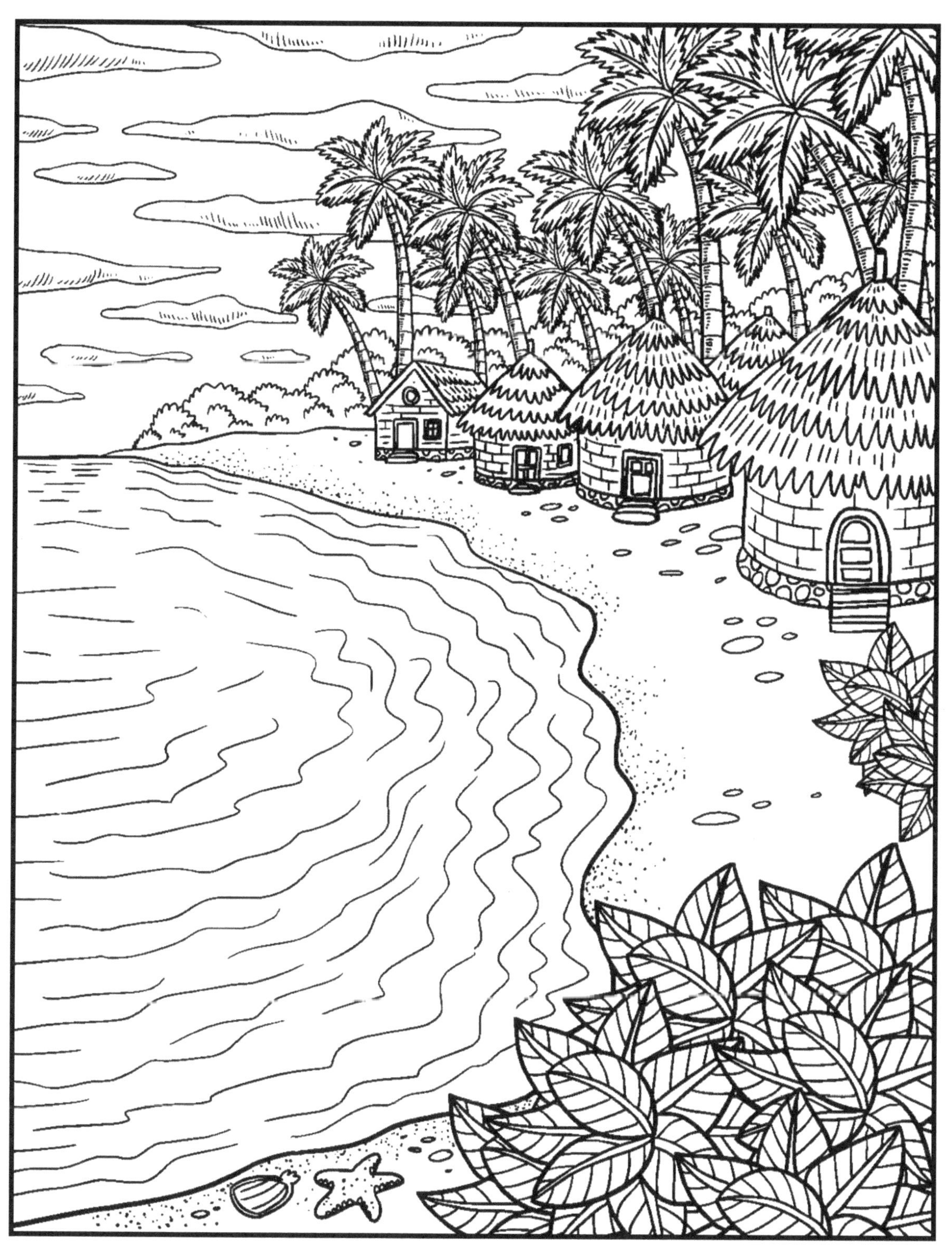

Life is short. Buy the ***beach house***.

ISLAND FUN!

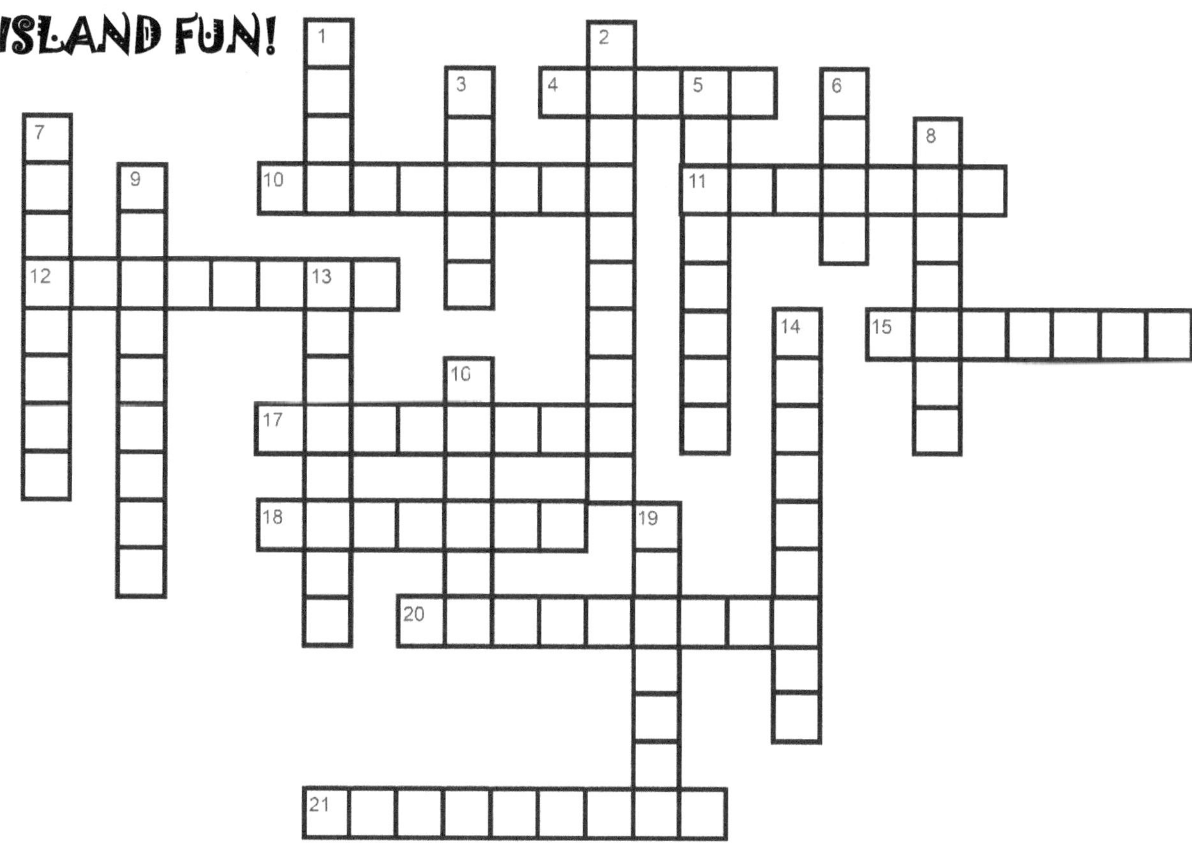

ACROSS

4. Sandy area that makes toes happy
10. An adornment one might find on a tropical beverage
11. To float while gazing underwater
12. Postcards From _____
15. Kindle and sparks of love on the island
17. Spirit animal found in this book
18. A traveler or one who visits
20. A tropical fruit
21. Thick, rooty, bushes that line the waterways

DOWN

1. A type of tropical tree
2. What one seeks to experience while on holiday
3. Go deep sea fishing in the _____
5. One who goes on a 3-hour tour and does not return
6. Wave activity; what one can do on the wave activity
7. Describes warm, humid climate
8. Vacation cuisine
9. Captain's helper
13. Relies heavily on the wind
14. Protection from the hottest planet
16. Itsy bitsy teeny weeny yellow polka-dot _____
19. Swimming danger due to water conditions

SUNBEAMS

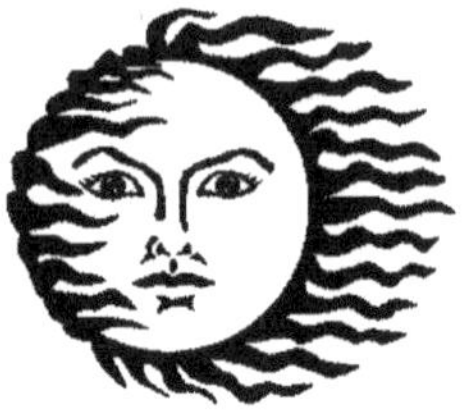

You are standing with your feet in the warm, soft sand at the edge of the water. The tide comes in and gently nudges your toes. Stare out into the ocean and ponder the underwater life that is teeming all around you. What deep thoughts come to you?

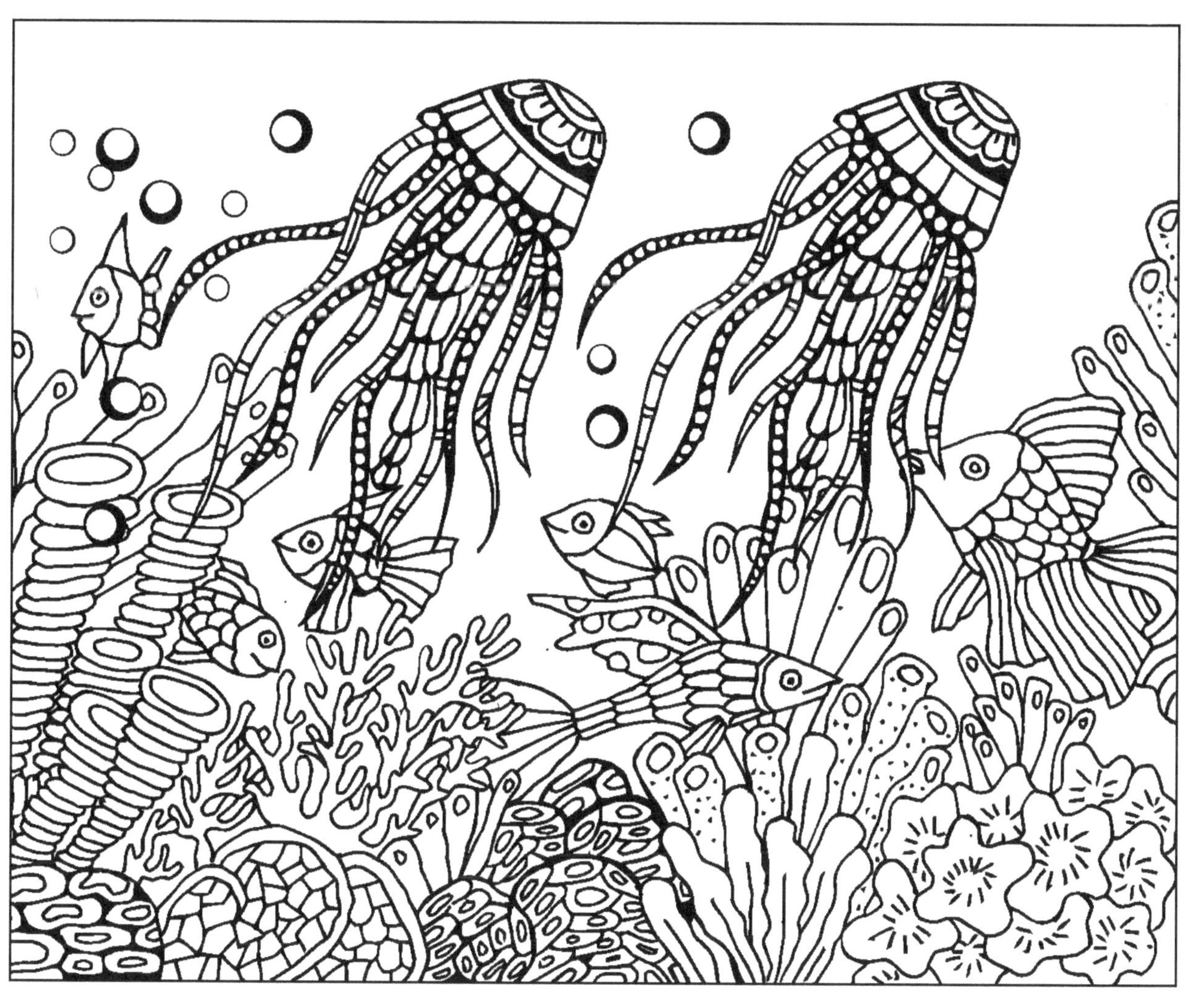

The serenity of the lulling ocean is a wondrous thing to behold...more precious than the gems covered in platinum or gold. ~Oksana Rus

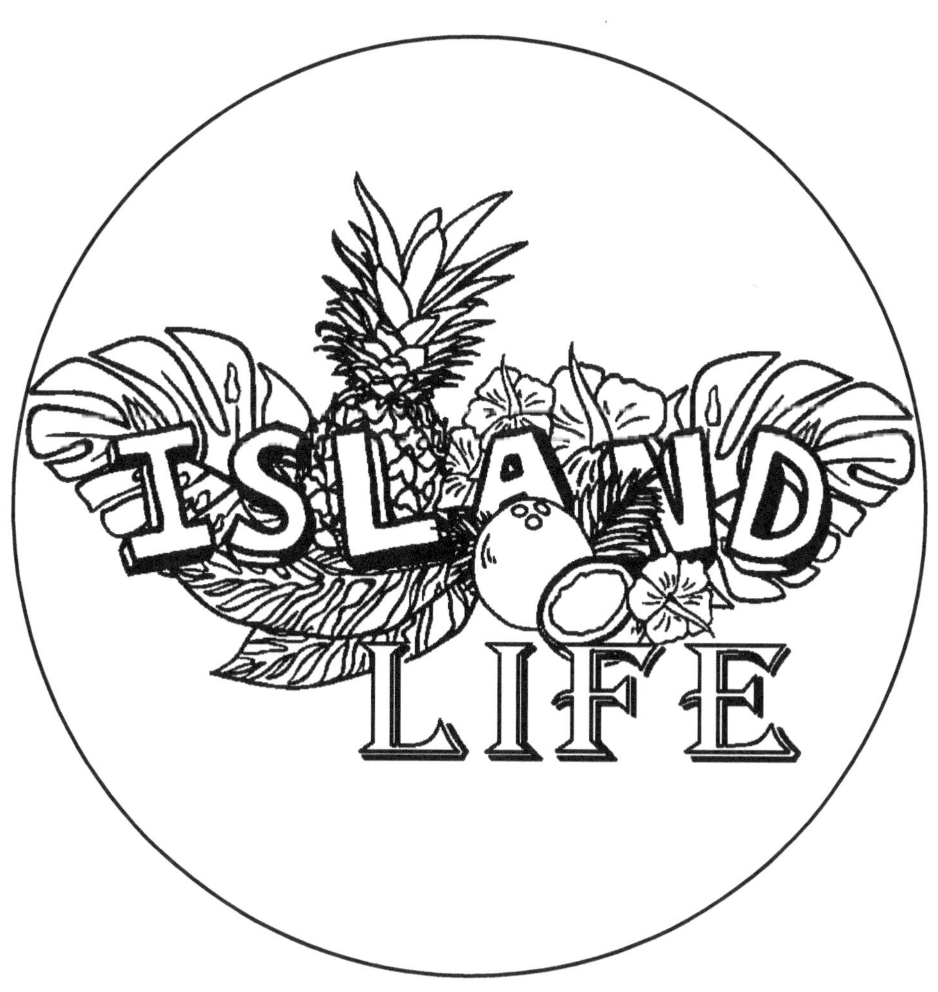

At the beach, LIFE is different. Time doesn't move hour to hour, but mood to moment. We live by the currents, plan by the tides and follow the Sun. ~Unknown

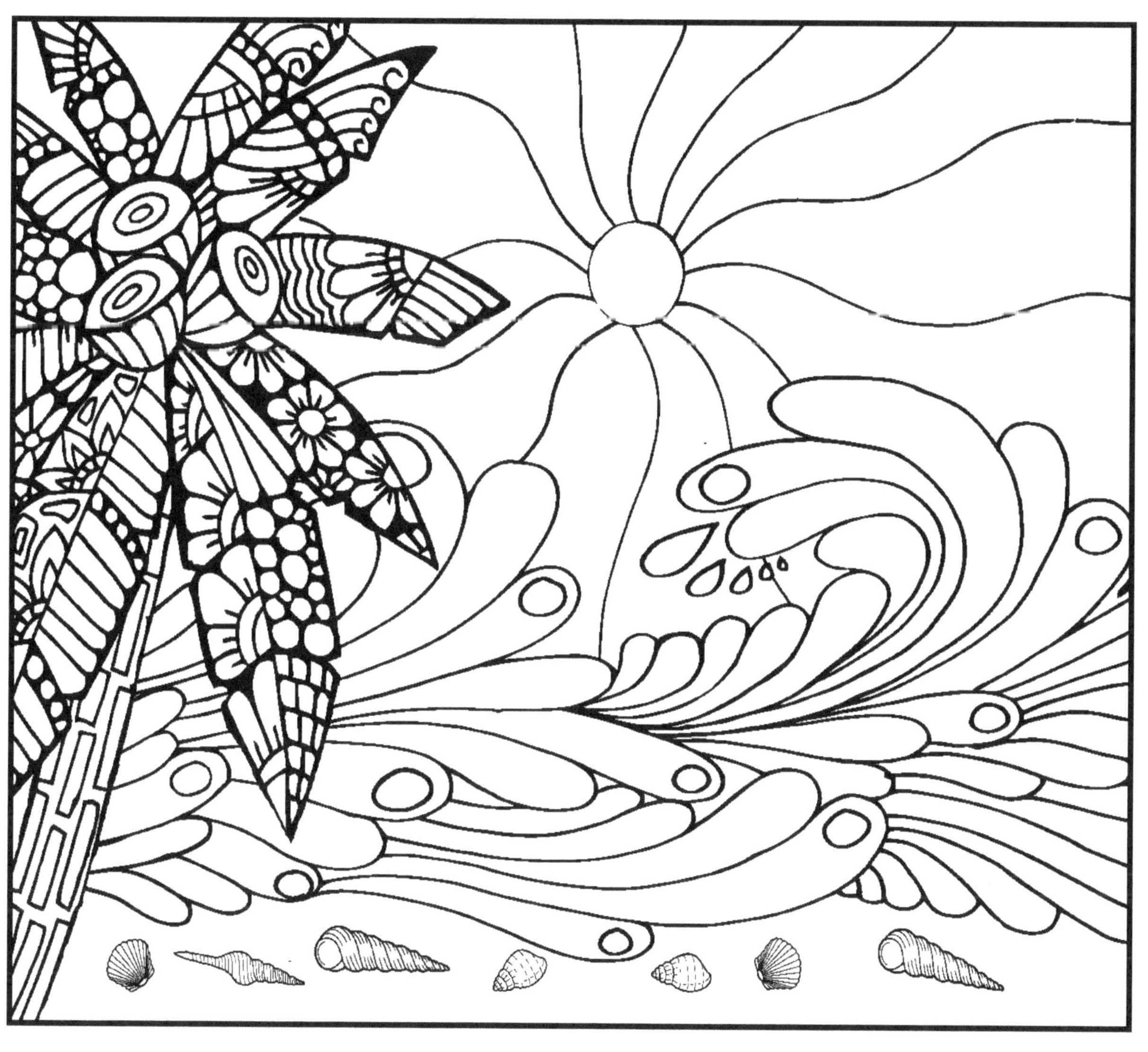

Live in the ***SUNSHINE****, swim the* ***SEA****, drink the* ***WILD AIR****.*

~Ralph Waldo Emerson

SUNBEAMS

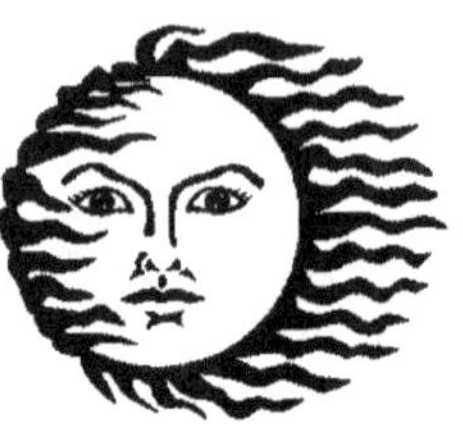

What would your family or friends say is your true calling?
Are they correct? What would ***you*** say is your true calling?
Describe the life of your dreams:

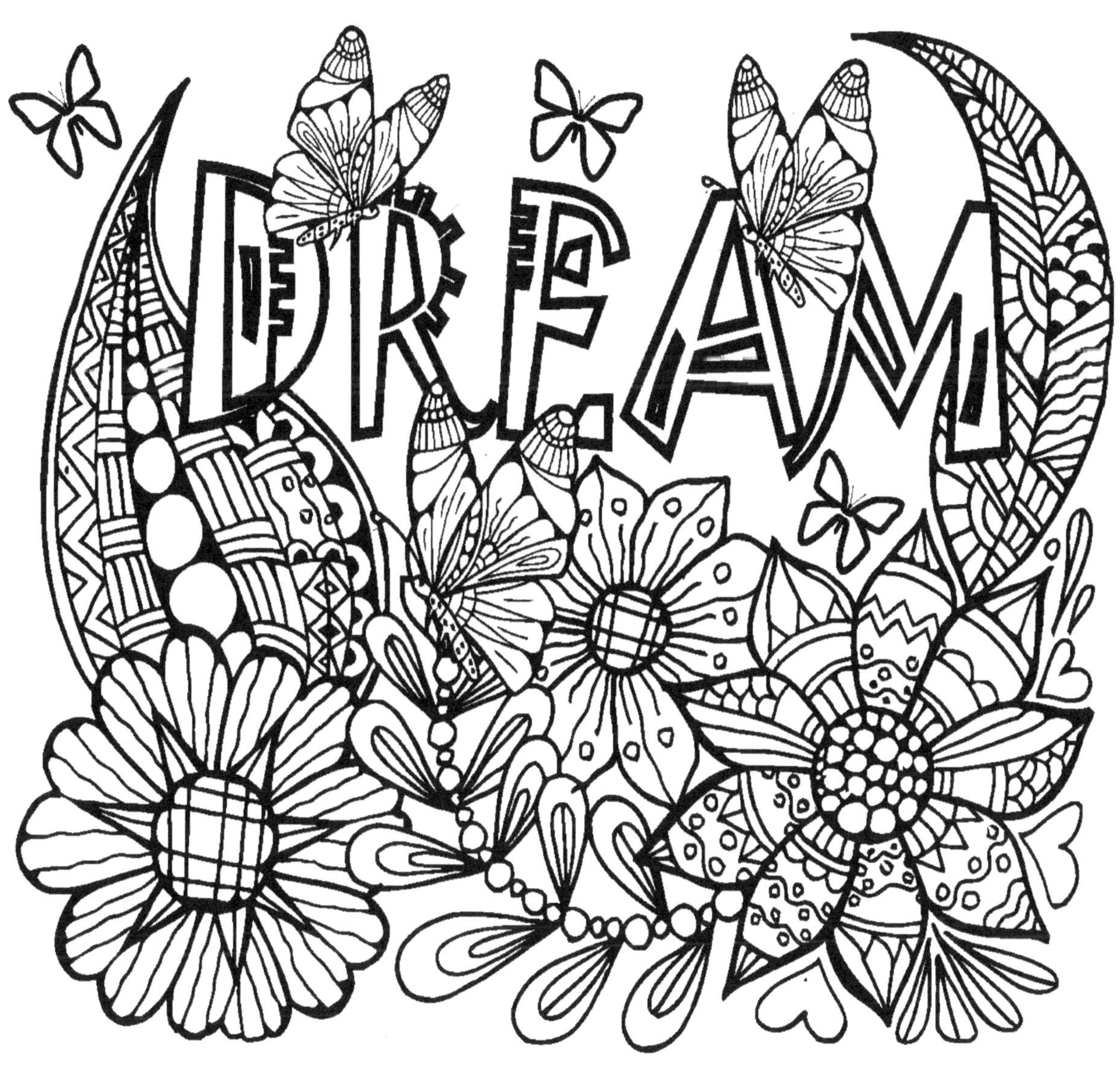

Affirmations:

I believe in the beauty of my dreams.

I believe in my abilities and intentions.

In my heart I know I can achieve that which I desire.

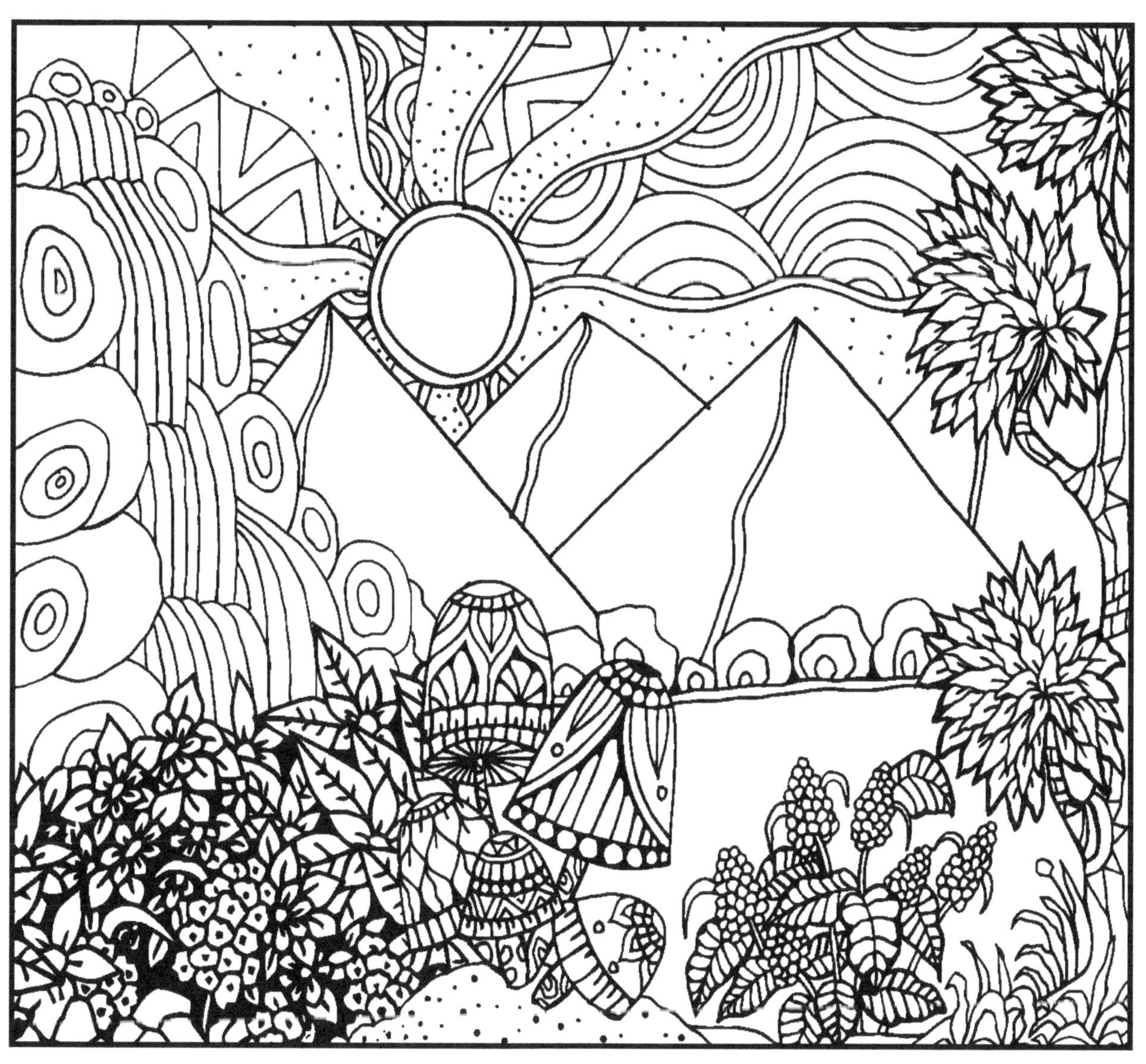

You're off to Great Places! Today is your day!
Your mountain is waiting. So...get on your way!

~Dr. Suess
Oh, The Places You'll Go!

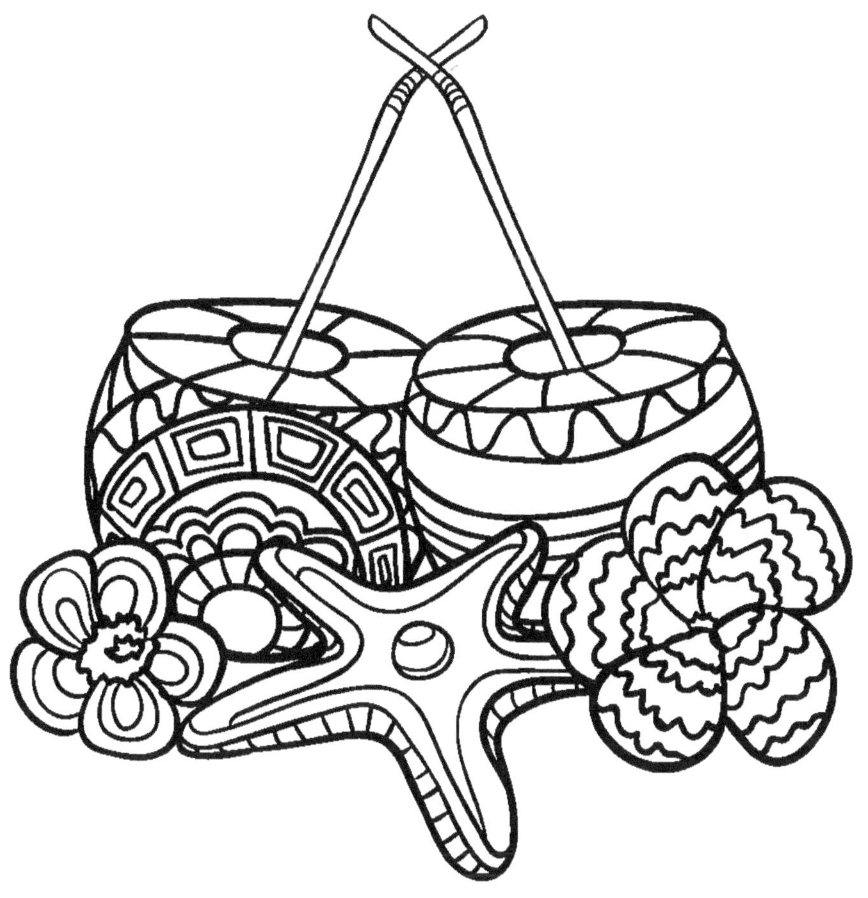

Offer me a sunny spot, a stunning view, and warm trade winds caressing my face. I listen only for the soothing sounds of the surf, and look for the hidden stars in the night sky, those made invisible by city lights. My toes in the sand, a fruity drink in my hand—and all is well in my world.

Tropical Trove Word Search

```
D H B F M O I R E N S Y B I G C S U G H V E
K S P E Y H C K E L S A Y E M Q Q D S K X L
R I Q G A Z L R E R T W N K A U A K J C M S
A F Y T W C C B E Y U S A D N C N D U V U D
L R O A I P H I N S I S A G A I H R O N V E
L A Q V T J N B A I C E B C R L S T S F S G
O T Z M Y E G N A W R E L D D I S E O I A L
D S O Z V N A N U L Y R Y Q O N T E G W P X
D G T U G U O K I B L T F N H S A U C C E P
N T O K G I L G G C I M S G O G H S O C K L
A S C I A N P L R U N L W Y I K R R N U J C
S P E L I C A N R T J A L D G P A A C A F A
R A B I K I T F H J X P D A M L I T H L W B
E S I D A R A P M O R F S D R A C T S O P A
S U N T A N L O T I O N E E N L Q G H F M N
S E V A W N A E C O S N E N U A E I E O A A
S U N G L A S S E S E F A L A A C Y L L B B
S P O L F P I L F V A A K C Y L B I L N U O
S V J X X S L O Q M G I N B U P P D S X C Y
T B N Z F F V B H F U D D D N O V A L U S G
N H G S P R D X O L L I G X L I T I E T M Y
V D V K T U S Q W G L H K F K Q C B L S A O
```

BEACH BALL
BEACH TOWEL
CABANA BOY
CONCH SHELL
CORAL REEF
FRUITY DRINKS
MUSIC AND DANCING
OCEAN WAVES
PALM TREES
PELICAN
POSTCARDS FROM PARADISE
RELAXATION
SAILBOAT
SAND CASTLE
SAND DOLLAR
SANDALS
SEAFOOD
SEAGULL
SEAPLANE
SNORKELING
SOUVENIRS
STARFISH
SUNGLASSES
SUNTAN LOTION
TIKI BAR
TOUCAN
TROPICAL VACATION

SUNBEAMS

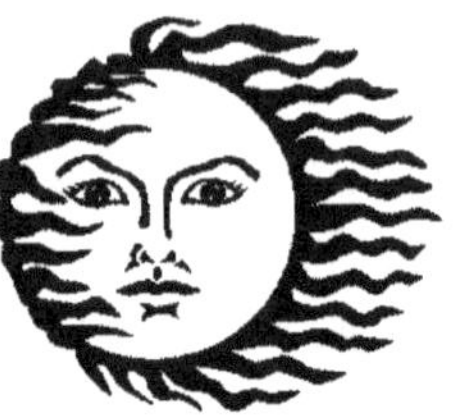

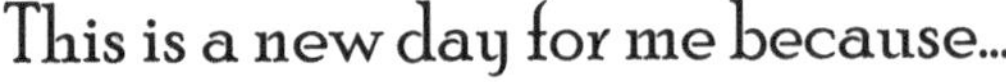
This is a new day for me because...

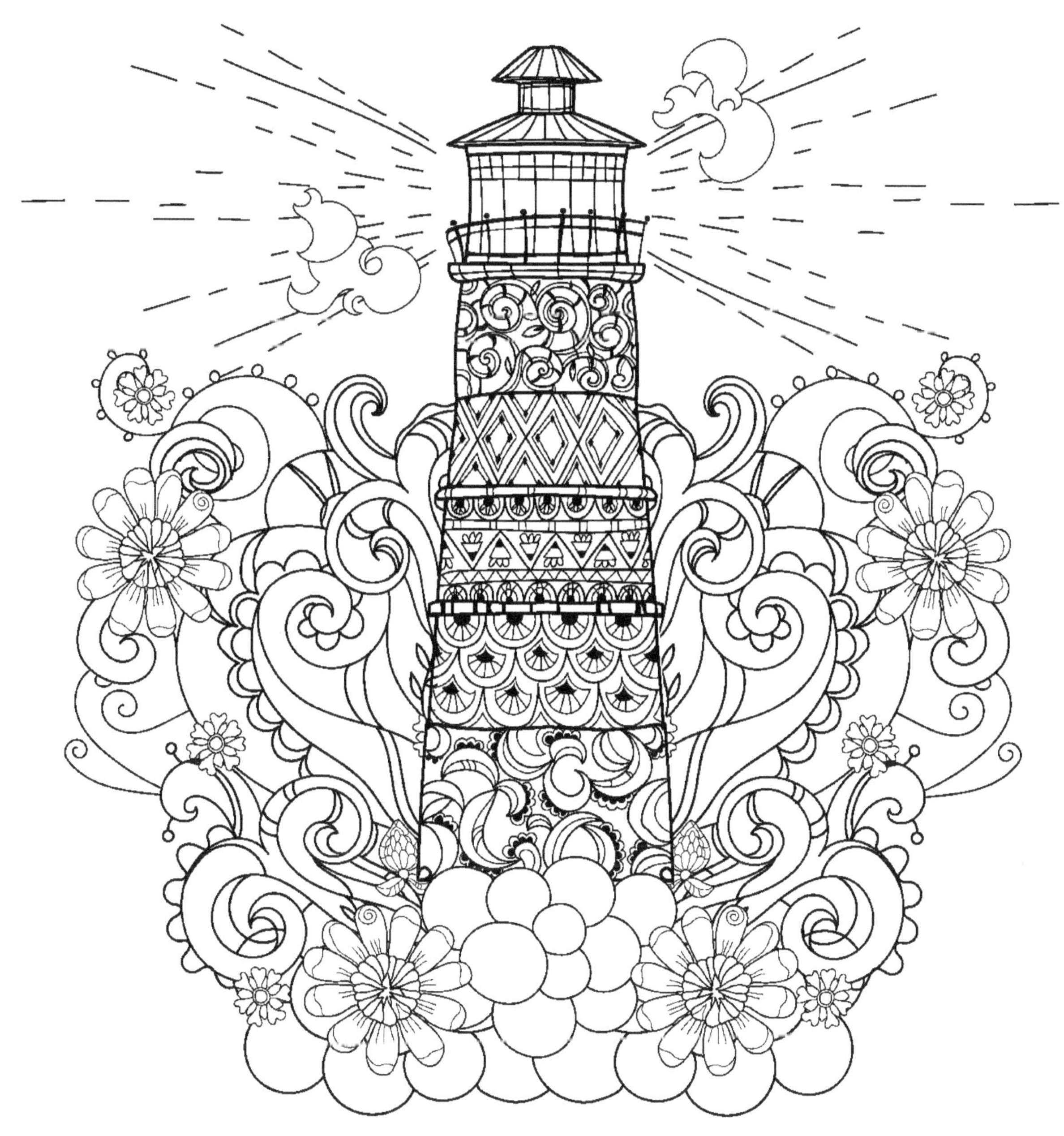

Lighthouses don't go running all over an island looking for boats to save; they just stand there shining. ~Anne Lamott

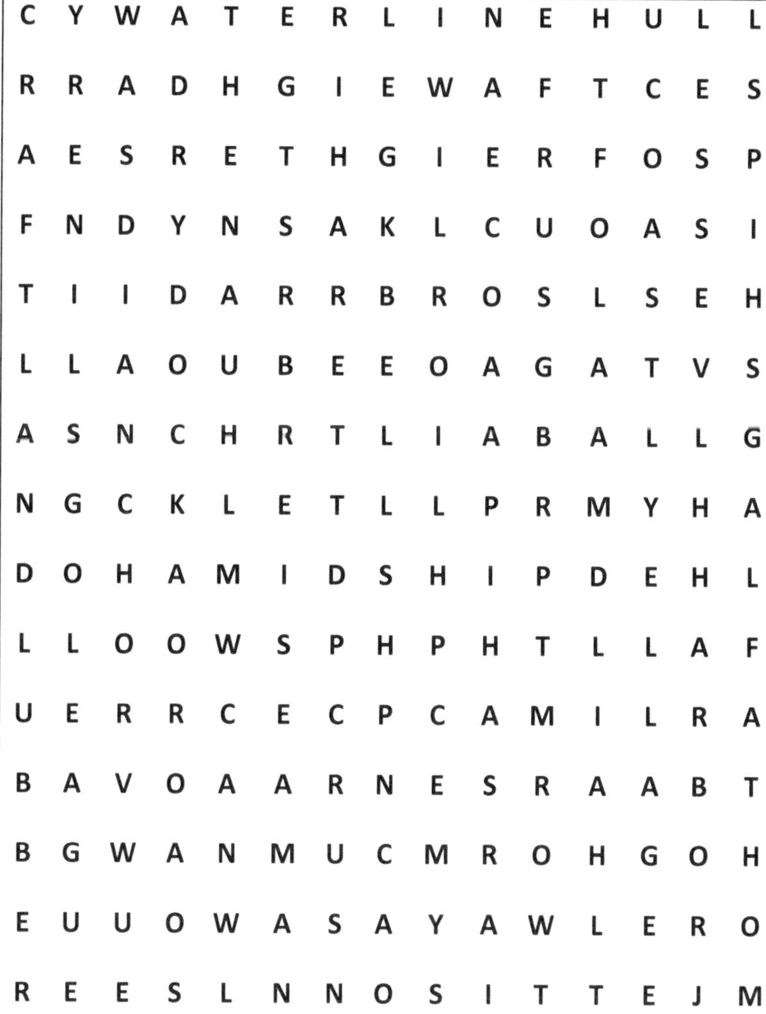

The SEAFARER

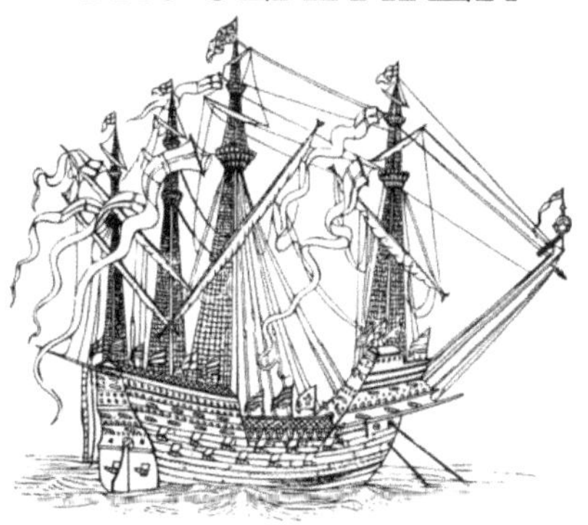

You are looking for a secret 11-letter word of unused letters. What is it?

____

Aboard
Aloft
Amidship
Anchor
Aweigh
Ball
Barometer
Bays
Canoe
Clipper
Coast
Craft

Crew
Drydock
Embark
Fathom
Flagships
Freighter
Galley
Hail
Harbor
Helmsman
Hull
Jettison

Landlubber
Launch
League
Liner
Logs
Maroon
Ocean
Piers
Pirate
Rudder
Sail
Scow
Scaman
Spar
Surf
Tiller
Vessel
Waterline
Wave
Wharf
Yarn
Yawl

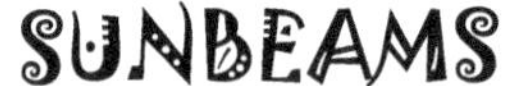

You just found a letter in a bottle. It is addressed to YOU. In the words of the late, great, singer/songwriter, Jim Croce, "*If I could save time in a bottle, the first thing that I'd like to do is*": (fill in the blank)

The Queen Conch

The conch (pronounced 'conk') shell has long been a symbol of grace and good fortune according to sailors throughout time. This beautiful shell is so indestructible that regardless of how stormy the sea, it remains intact. It is a symbol of strength and endurance—not only against the sea, but against the stormy seas of life as well. It is said that if you hold it to your ear, you can hear the call of the ocean once again. Listen carefully as you color. What message does she bring you today?

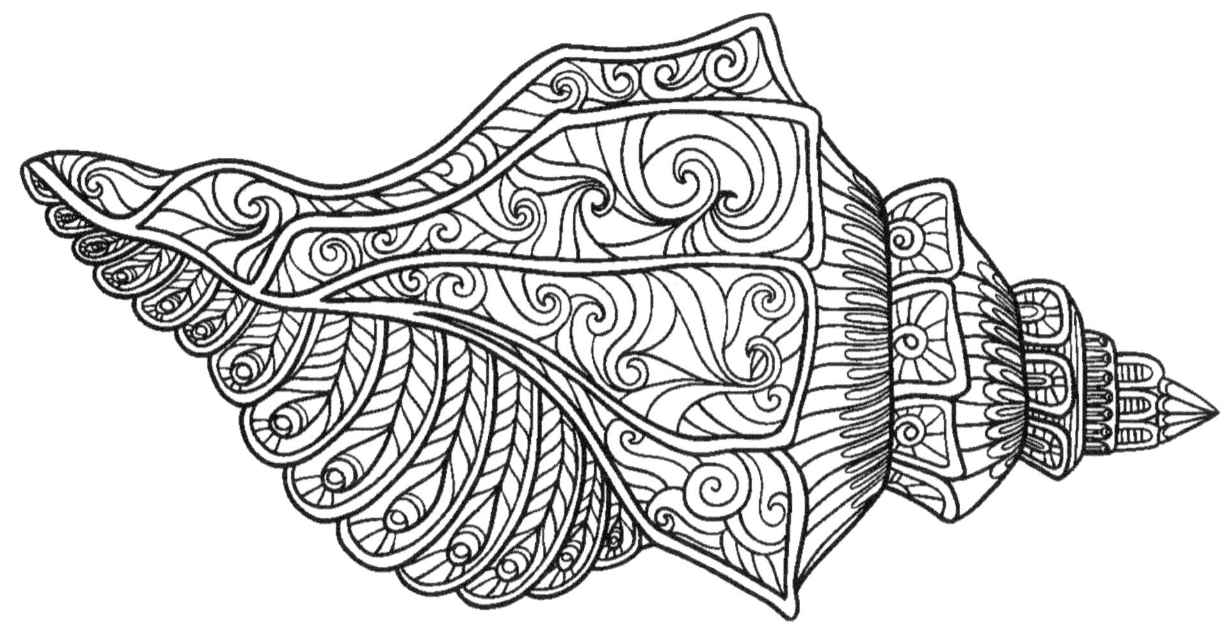

Sea Boho
collection

The Dolphin

The deep blue sea spoke to me,
it was holding back a mystery.
A dolphin took me by the hand,
it wanted me to understand:
That in this life there is more to behold
than bags of money and pots of gold.
Believe in yourself and you will see
how happy and free you were meant to be.
~ Author Unknown

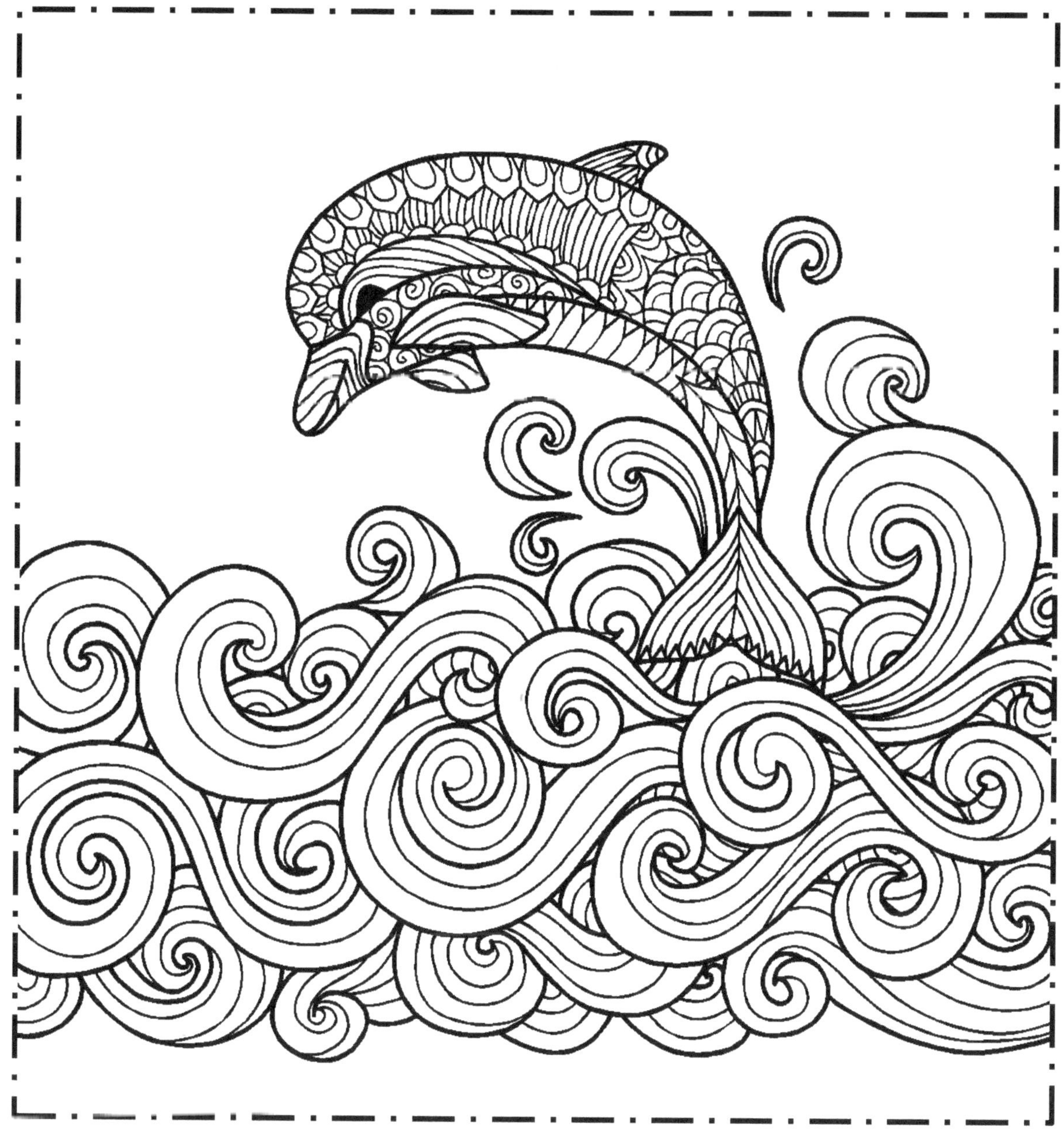

I alone cannot change the world but I can cast a stone across the waters to create many ripples. ~Mother Teresa

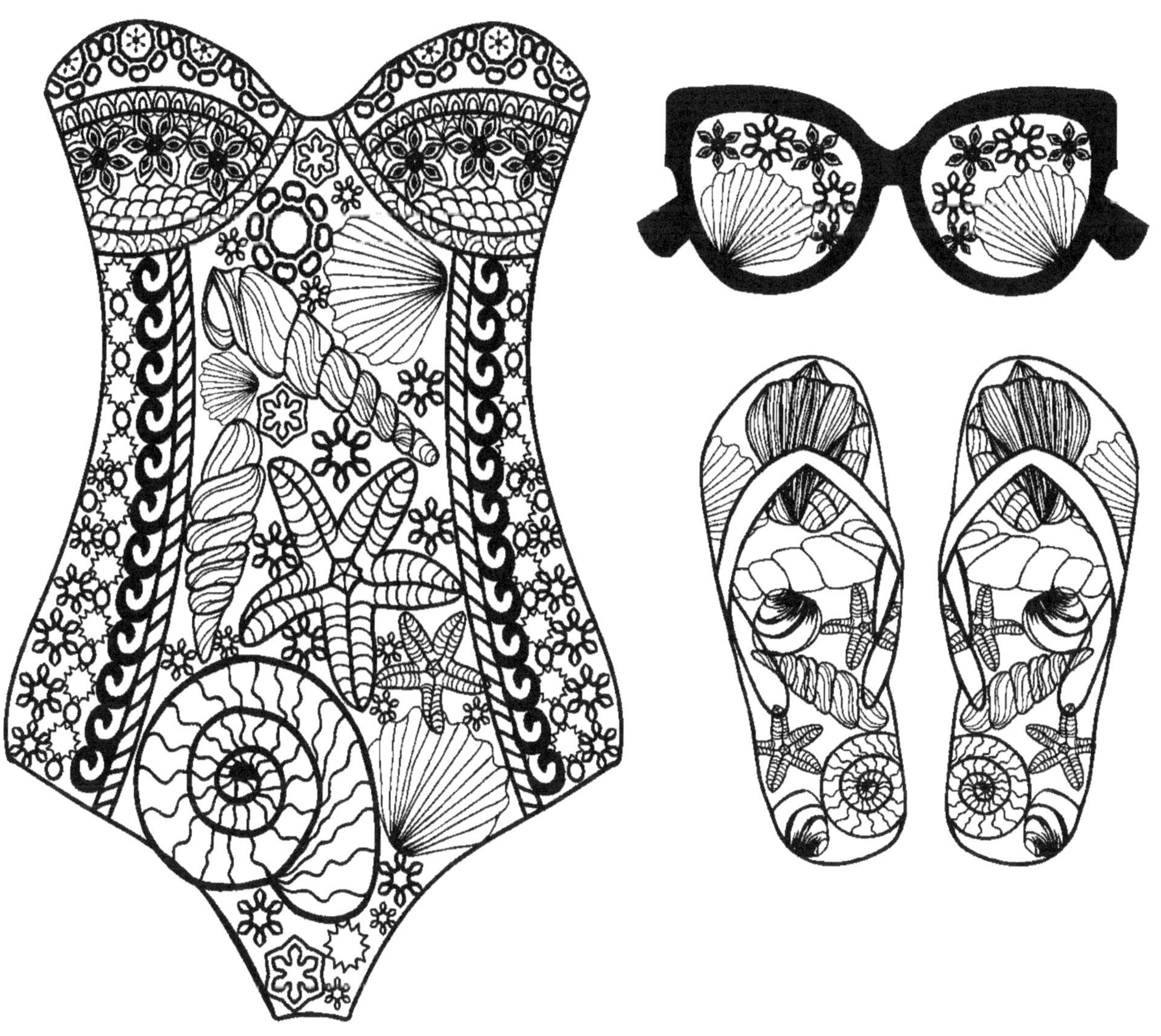

The best color in the whole world is the one that looks good on **YOU**!

~Coco Chanel

SUNBEAMS

Take a snapshot back in time. Time stands still for you now.

What era did you revisit? Where did you go? Who waits for you there? Trace your footsteps back...

Take only memories...

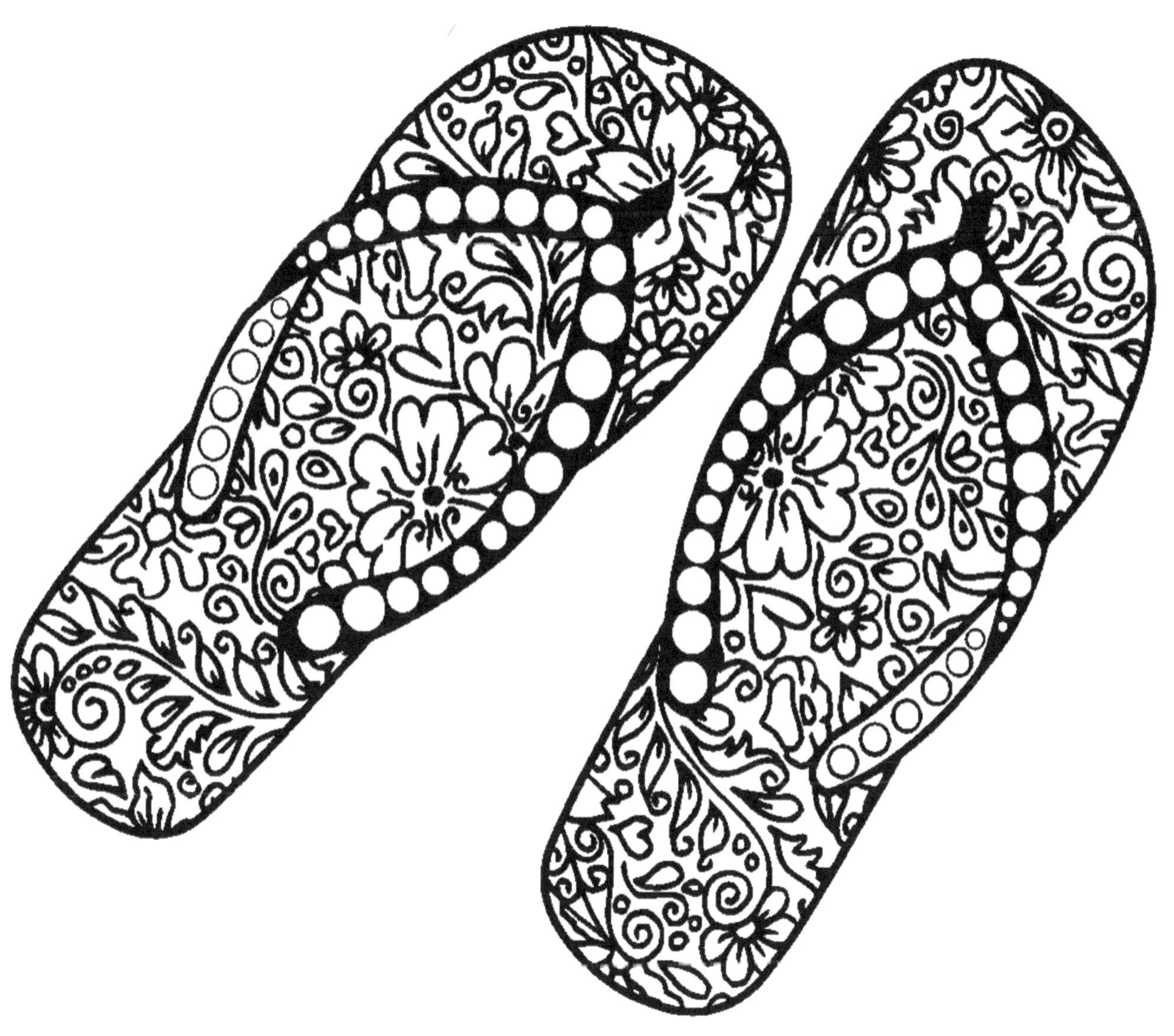

...Leave only footsteps.

~Chief Seattle

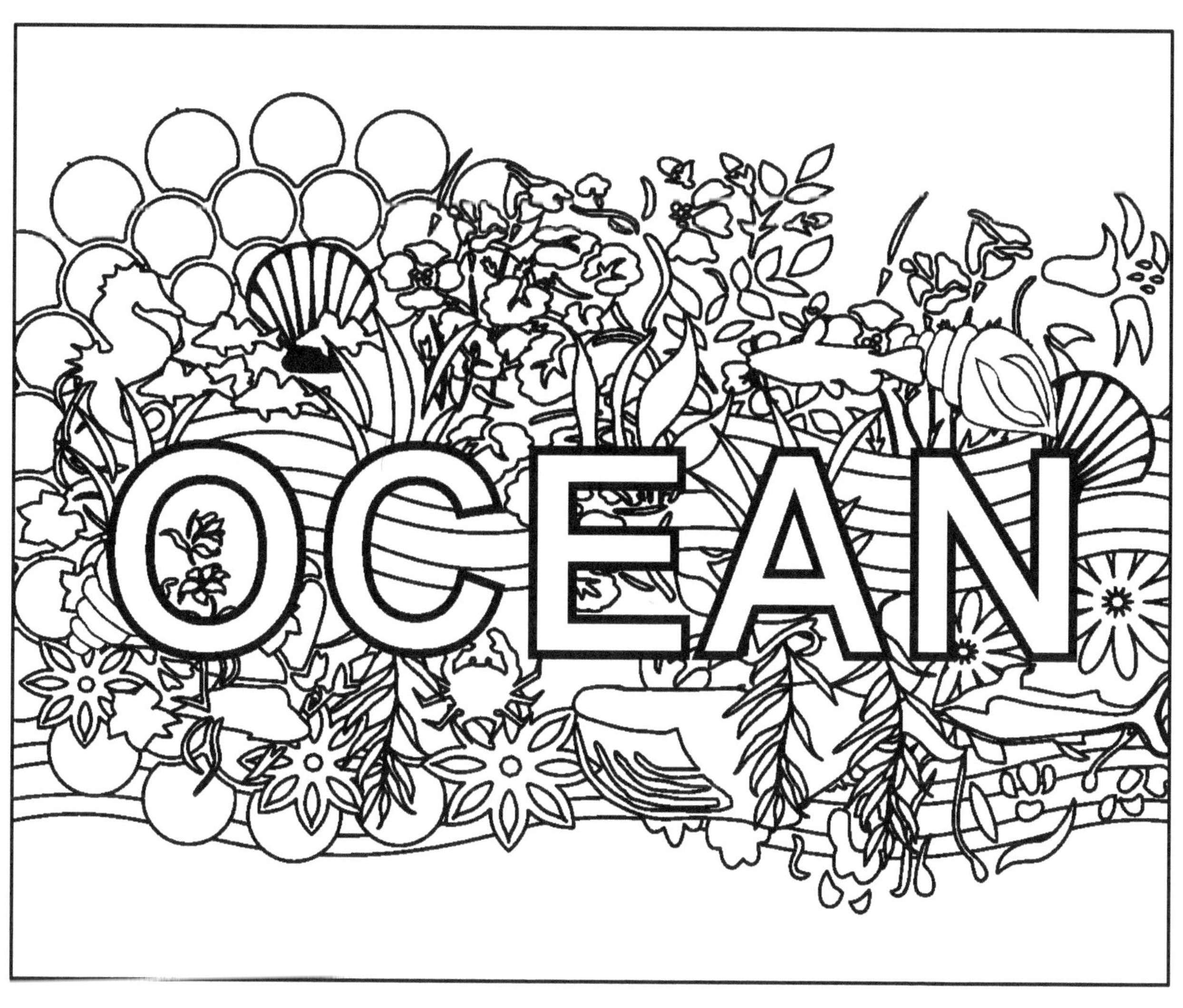

The sea, once it casts its spell, holds one in its nets forever.

~Jacques Cousteau

SUDOKU

#1 EASY RIDER
(EASY)
NOTES:

5	4		7		8			2
	1			2		4		7
2	9		4	5				8
	6	2						5
3				6				9
9						3	1	
4				7	2		8	1
8		6		4			2	
7			8		5		9	4

#2 TIPSY TOURIST
(MEDIUM)
NOTES:

3								1
	8		3	2		5		9
1			4		6	7		3
	4				8		2	
				3				
	7		6				9	
8		1	5		4			2
4		5		9	7		3	
7								5

#3 GLOBETROTTER
(DIFFICULT)
NOTES:

					4			1
	3			1		8		7
	1		7				9	
		6					4	
		3	2		7	5		
	8					1		
	4				9		3	
3		5		2			7	
2			6					

#4 JETSETTER
(CHALLENGER)
NOTES:

						3	8	
	5						2	6
9			6					
	1			6		4		2
		2	3		7	6		
7		8		1			5	
					4			5
4	9						6	
	7	3						

Sentence Scramble Challenge

Use the following sets of letters to complete the sentences below. For example, you will see sets of letters such as: **OTH AYI ISE. ERD NPA TAN JUS RAD**

If you rearrange them like this: **JUS TAN OTH ERD AYI NPA RAD ISE**., you will arrive at this quote: **JUST ANOTHER DAY IN PARADISE**. Ready to try? Punctuation marks are included as landmarks to help you get started.

ACK;	**ERE**	**NGL**	**TAR**
ART	**ERE**	**NNO**	**TED**
ATW	**ERH**	**NTL**	**THE**
AVI	**GBA**	**NWE**	**THE**
CKT	**HOW**	**OFW**	**THE**
COM	**IFF**	**OTH**	**TRA**
EAP	**ISI**	**OUR**	**VEL**
EARE.	**LDD**	**OWH**	**WAY**
EAS	**MEB**	**RAV**	**WES**
ECA	**MIN**	**SAM**	**WET**
EFT.	**NCO**	**SBE**	**WOR**
ELS	**NEV**	**SEE**	**Y.CO**

__ ______ __ ____ __ ___ ____ ____; ____

__ ___ ___ _____ ___________. ______ ____

__ _____ __ _______ __ __ __ ___ ___ ____

__ _____ ______ ____. __________ ______ _

____ __ ___ __ ___.

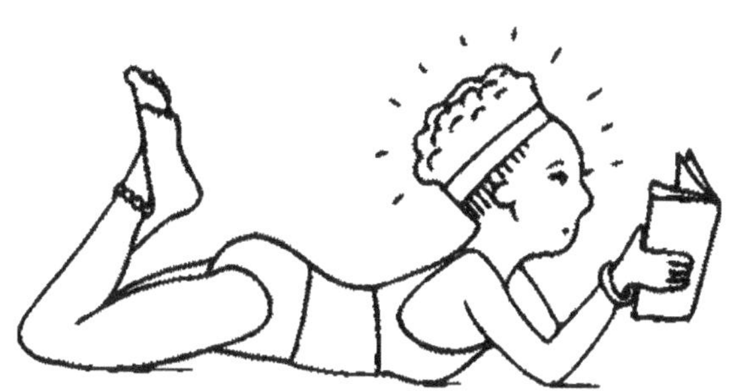

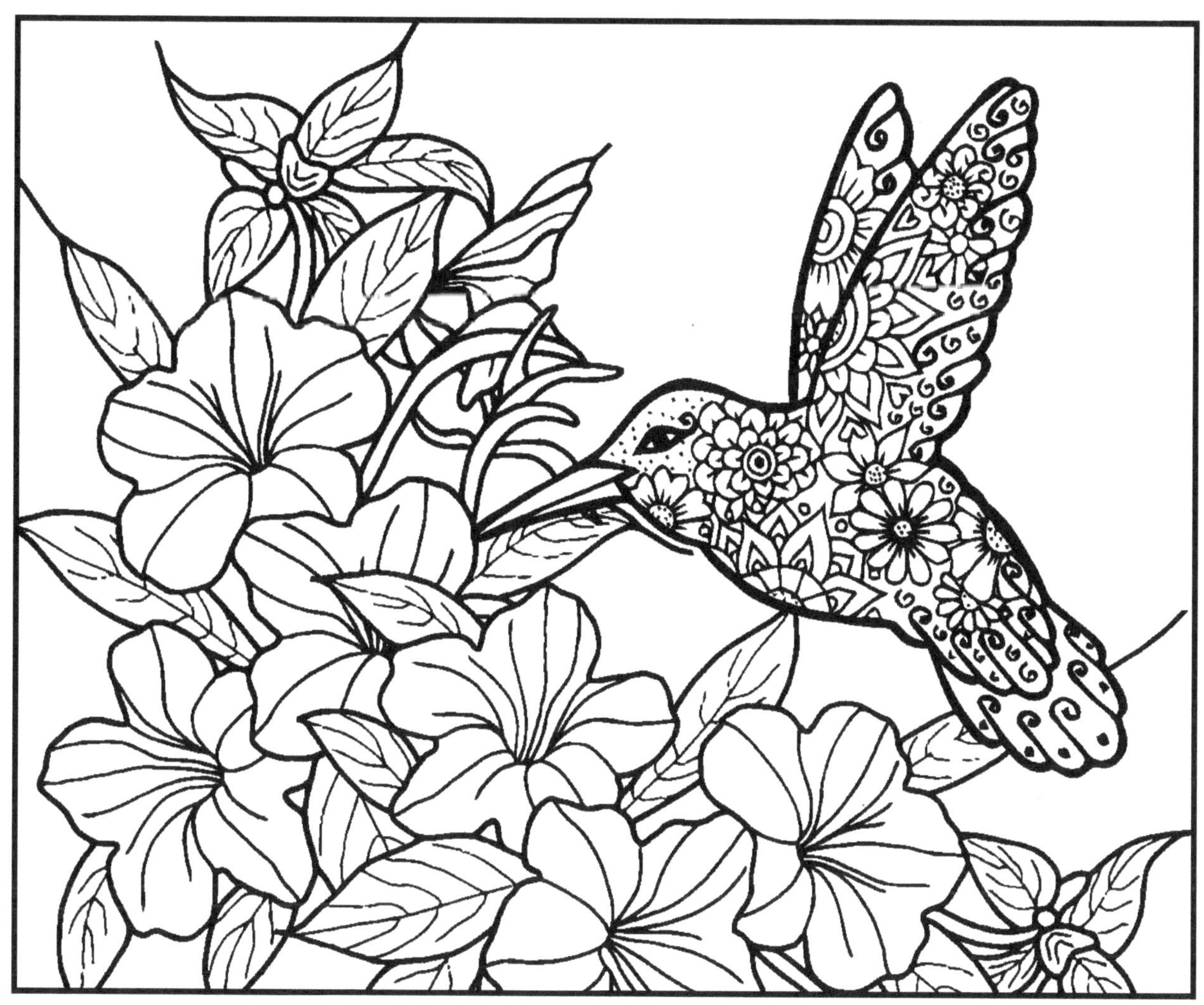

Affirmation:

I pause to hover when needed. I seek delight in the smallest things in life. The sweetest nectar I will ever find has already been gifted to me and lives within me now. I am free to be ME.

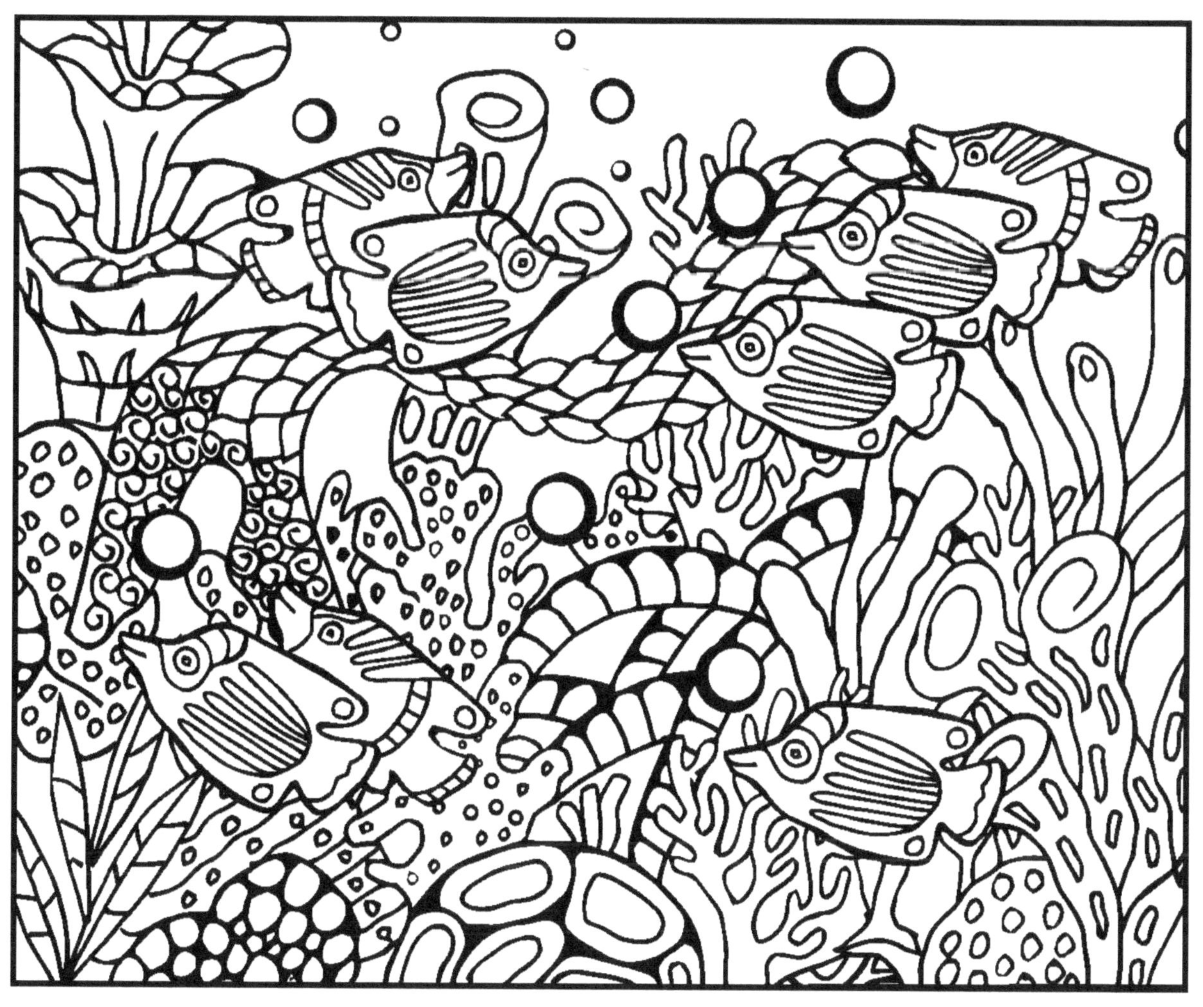

Many men go fishing all of their lives without knowing that it is not fish they are after.

~Henry David Thoreau

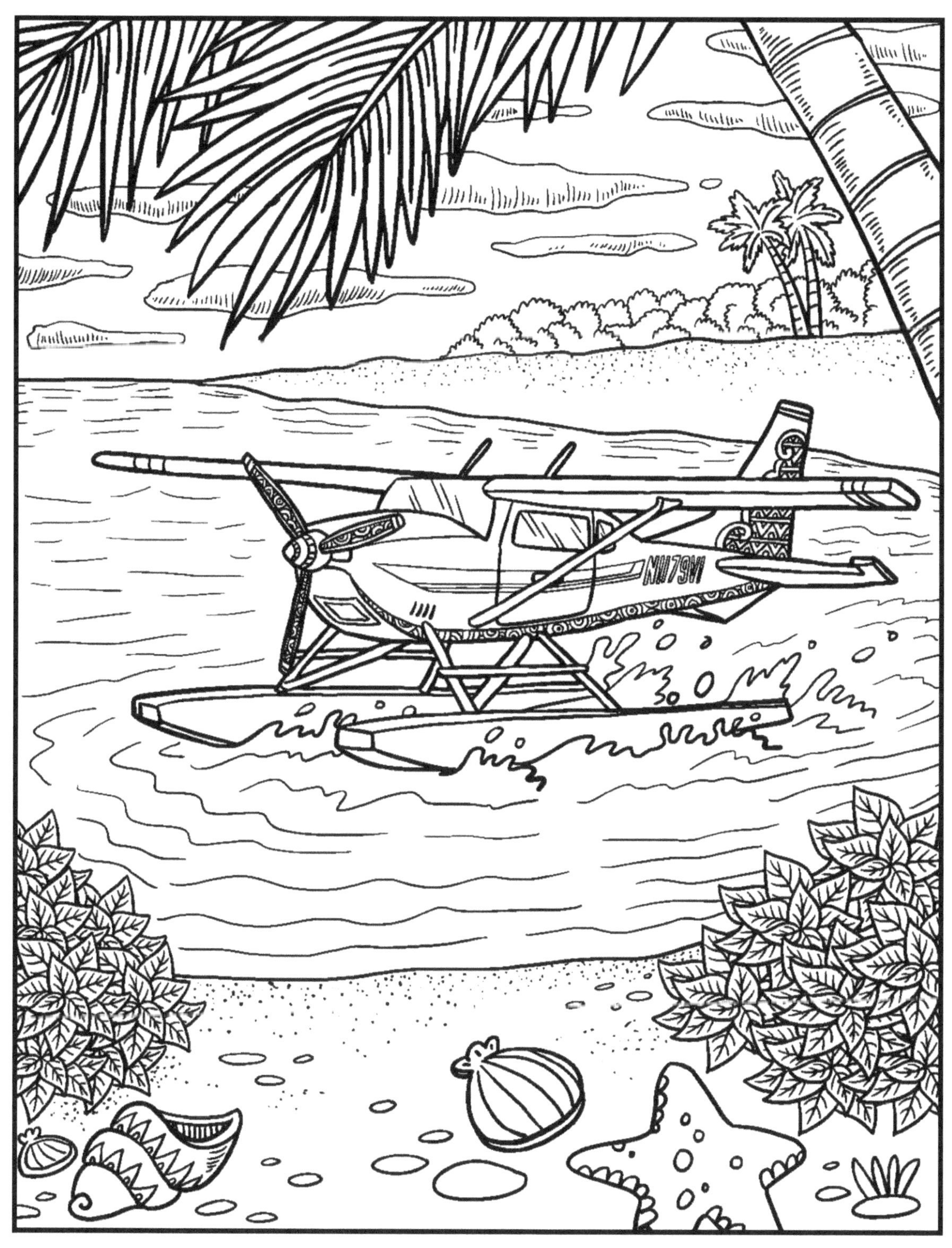

Life is either a daring adventure or nothing.
~Helen Keller

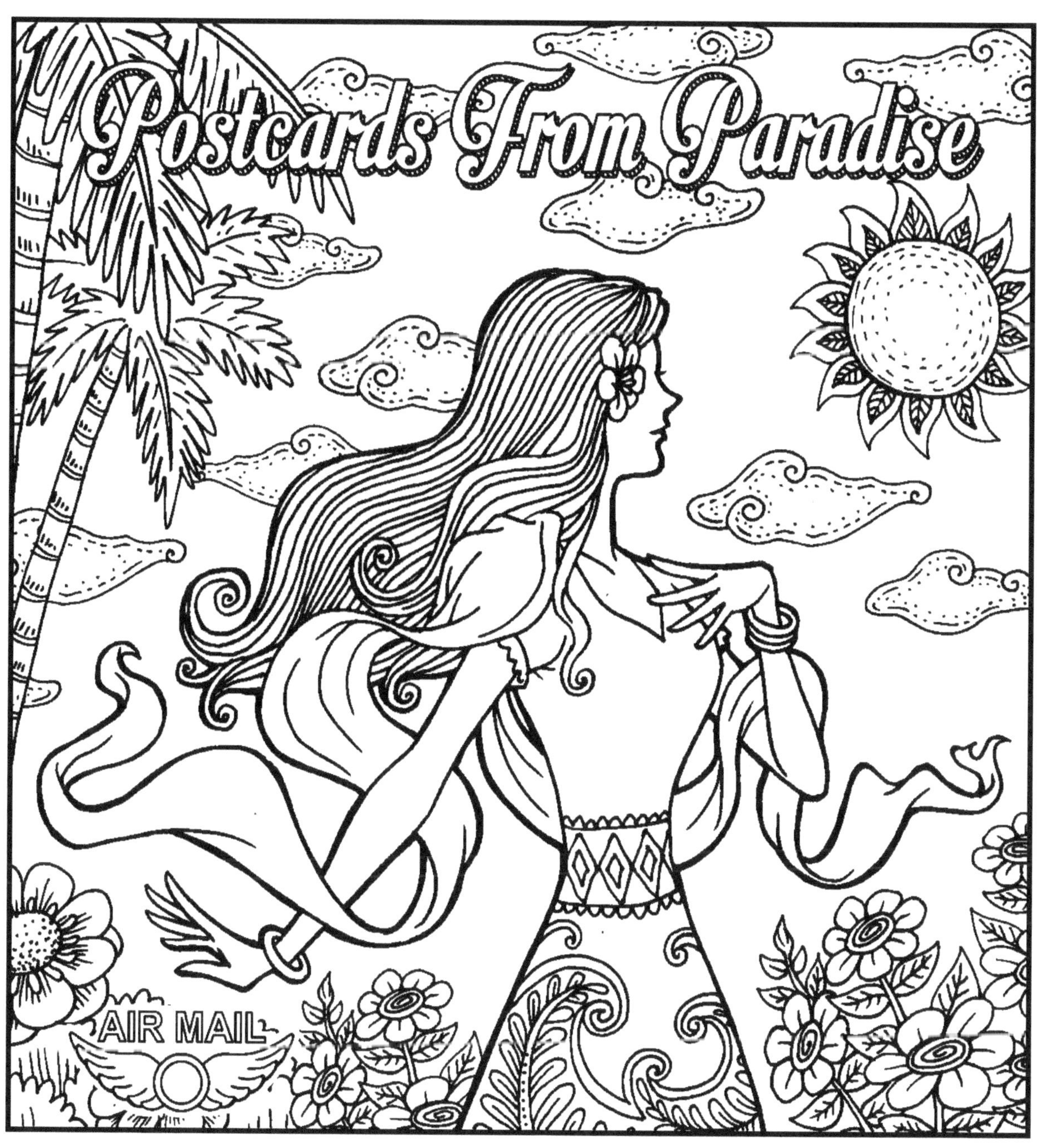

Paradise isn't a place—it's a state of mind. So, take **your paradise** *wherever you travel. Pack it in your carry-on, and carry on.*

~Connie Gorrell

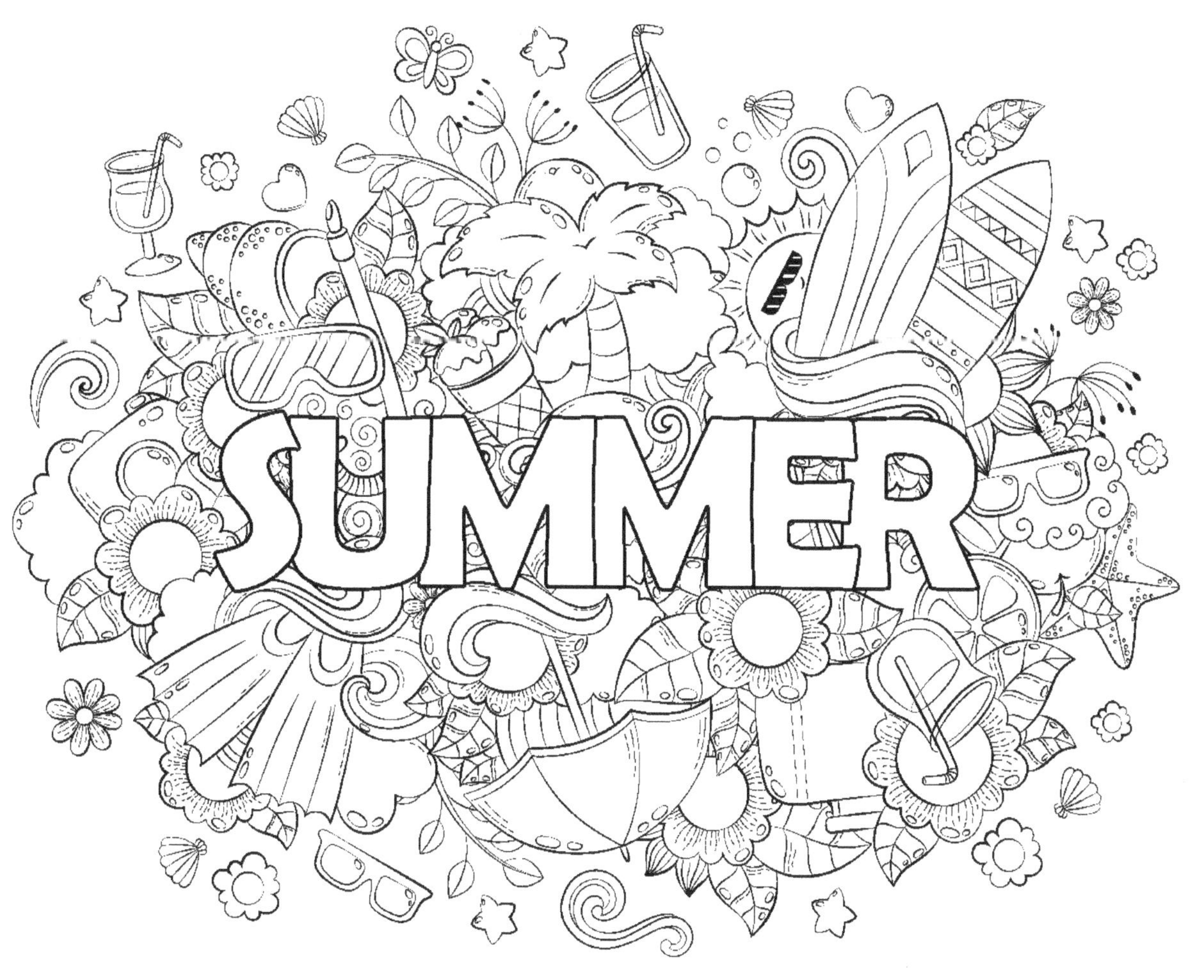

Summertime is always the best of what might be.

~ Charles Bowden

SUNBEAMS

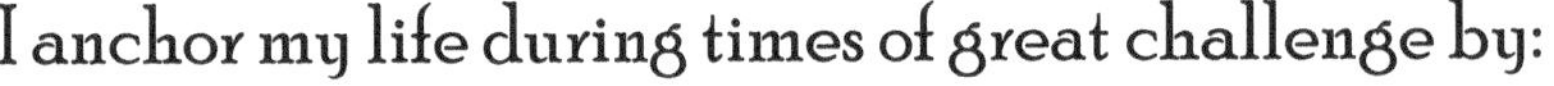

I anchor my life during times of great challenge by:

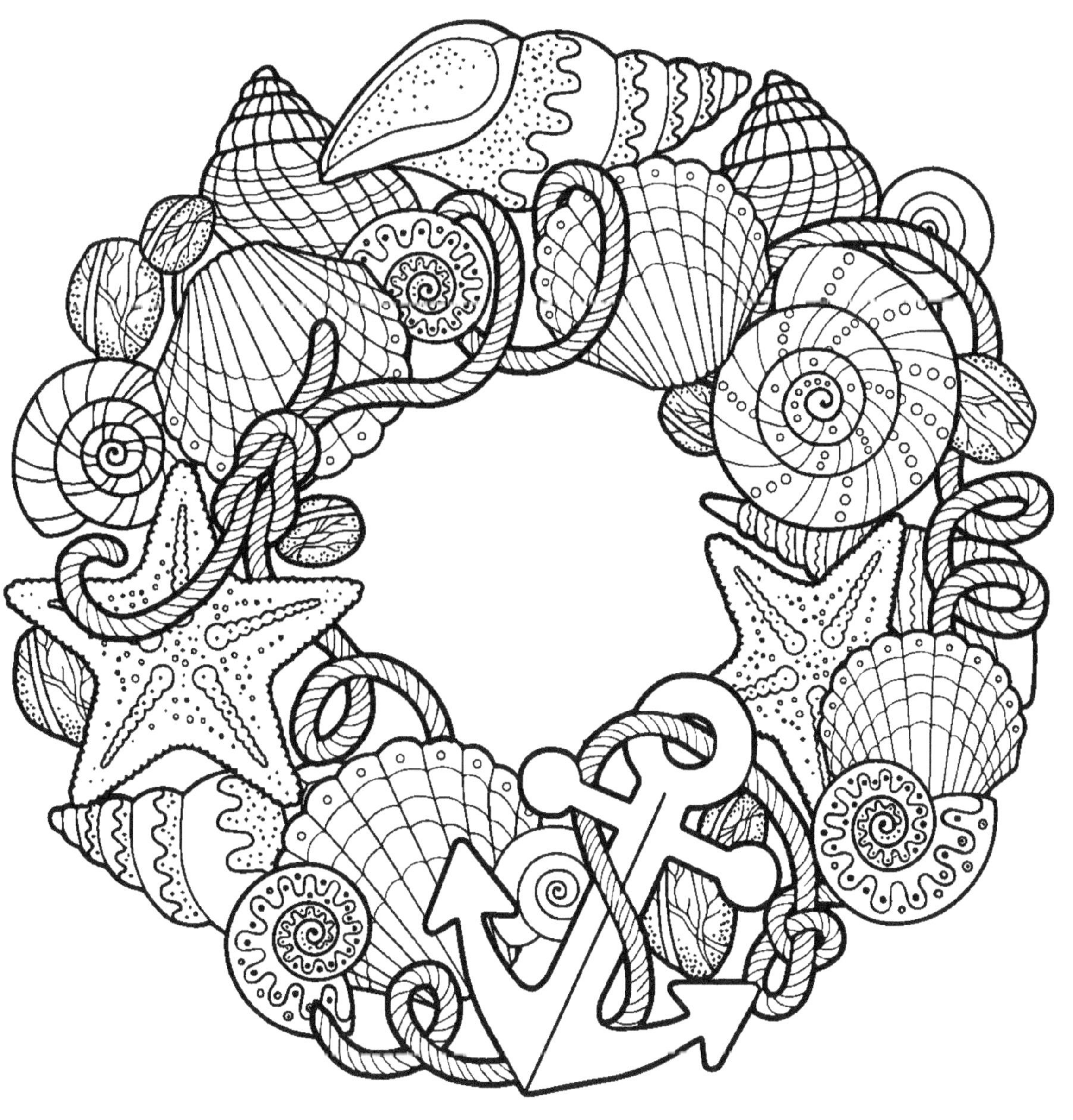

In order to realize the worth of the anchor, we need to feel the stress of the storm.

~Corrie ten Boom

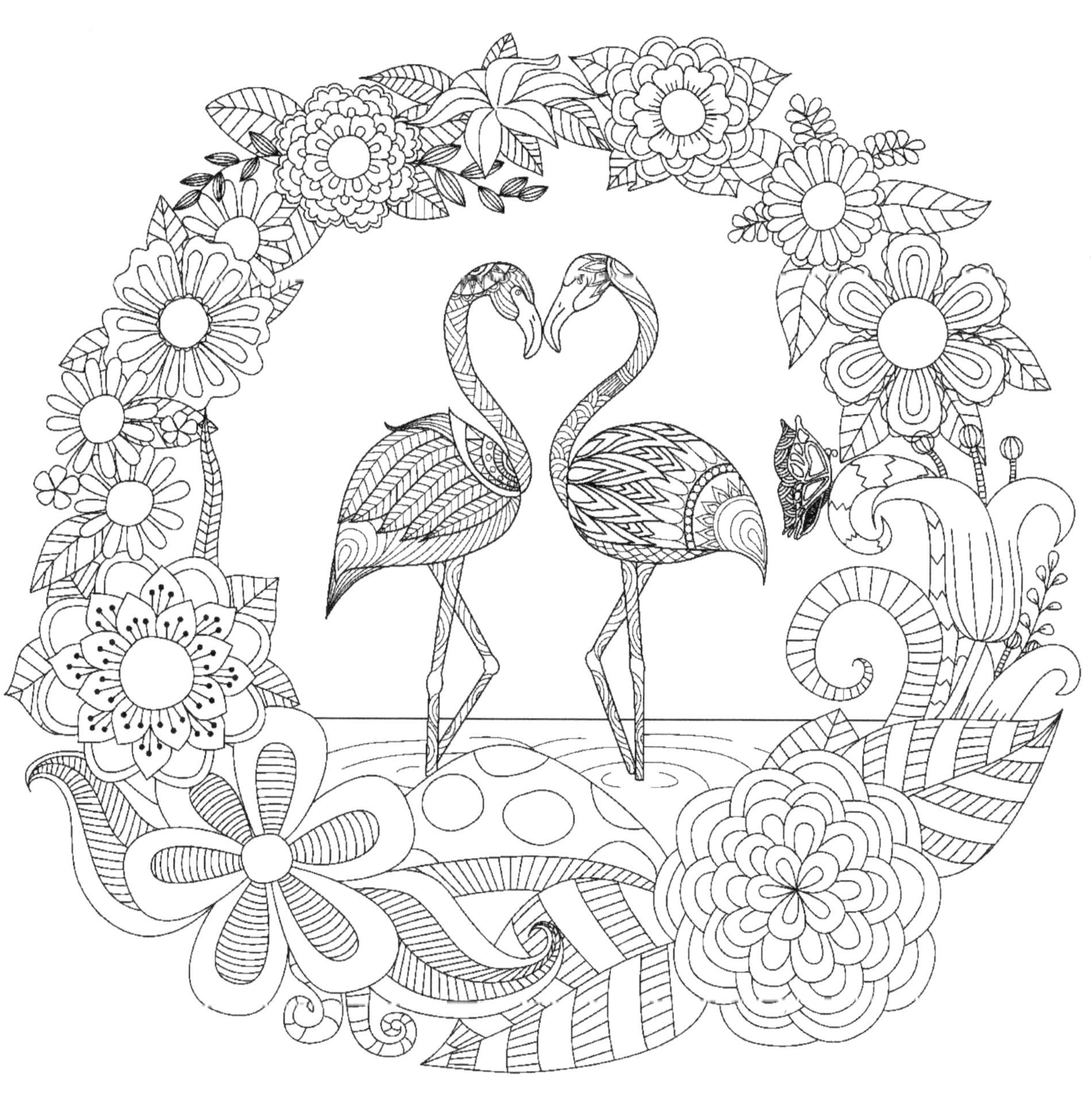

Pink lawn **flamingos** are my **spirit animal**.

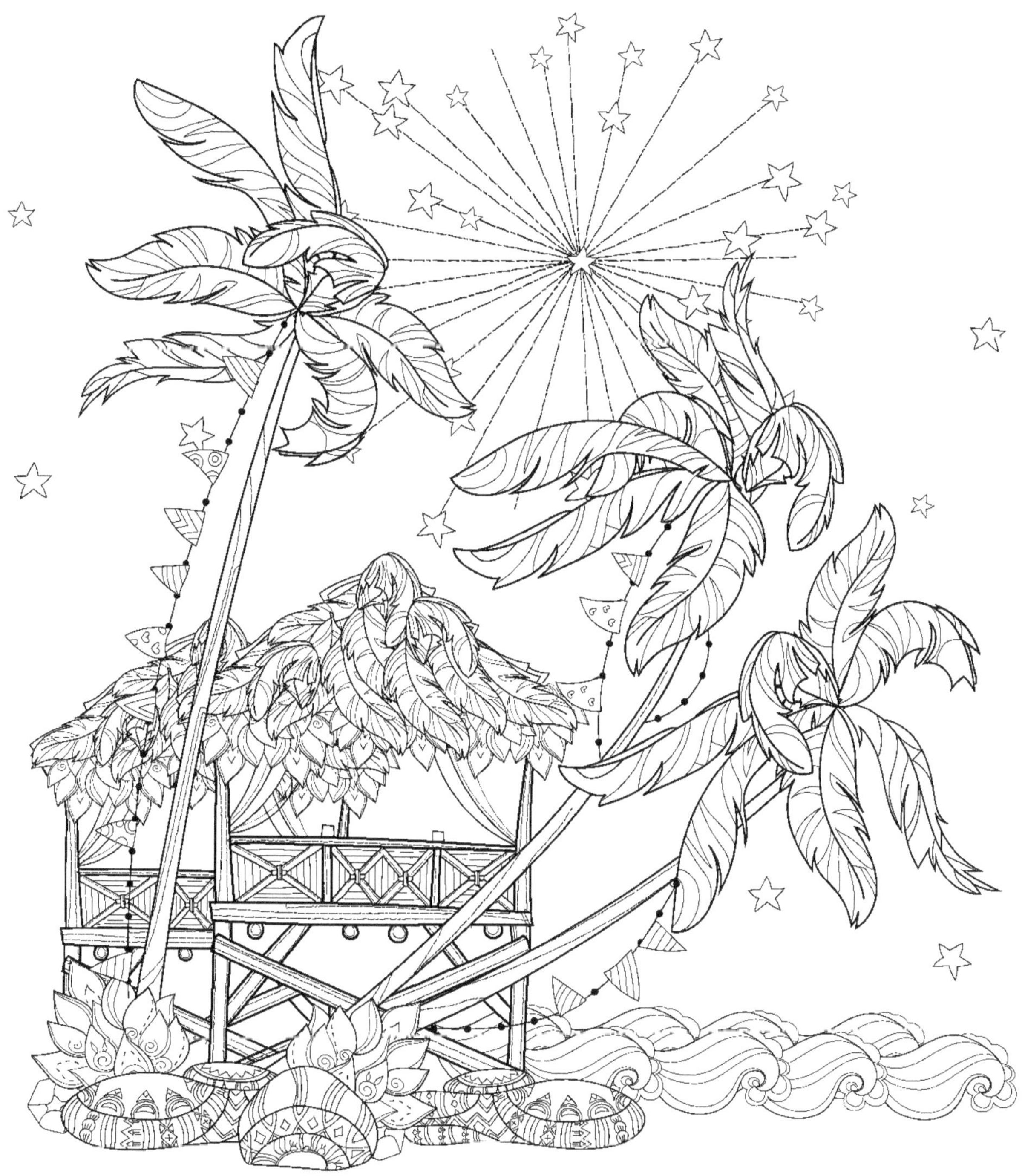

Palm trees, ocean breeze, salty air, sun kissed hair.

Oh, my **Paradise**! Take me there!

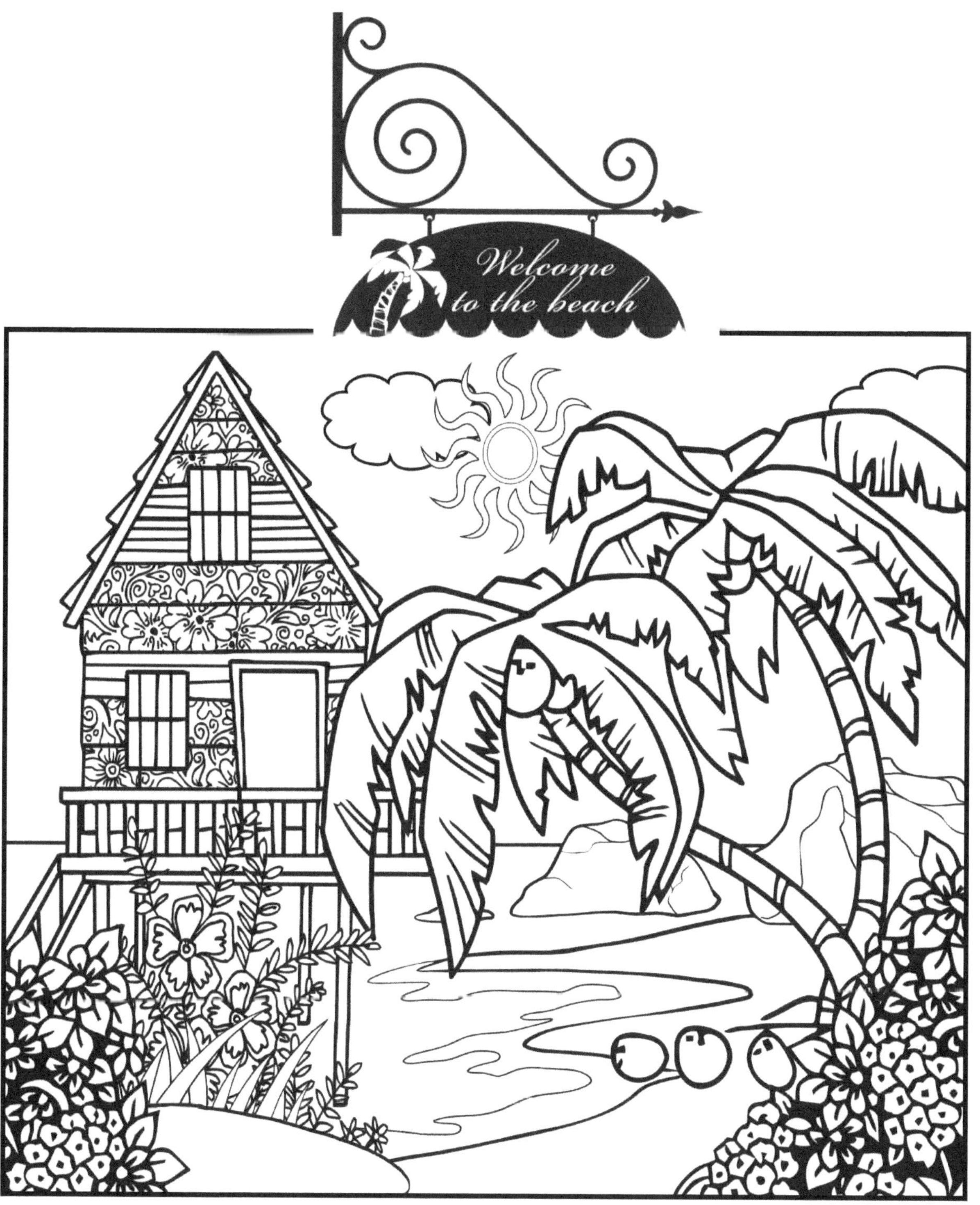

Home is where the **beach** is.

DOODLE PAGE

Add your favorite beach items

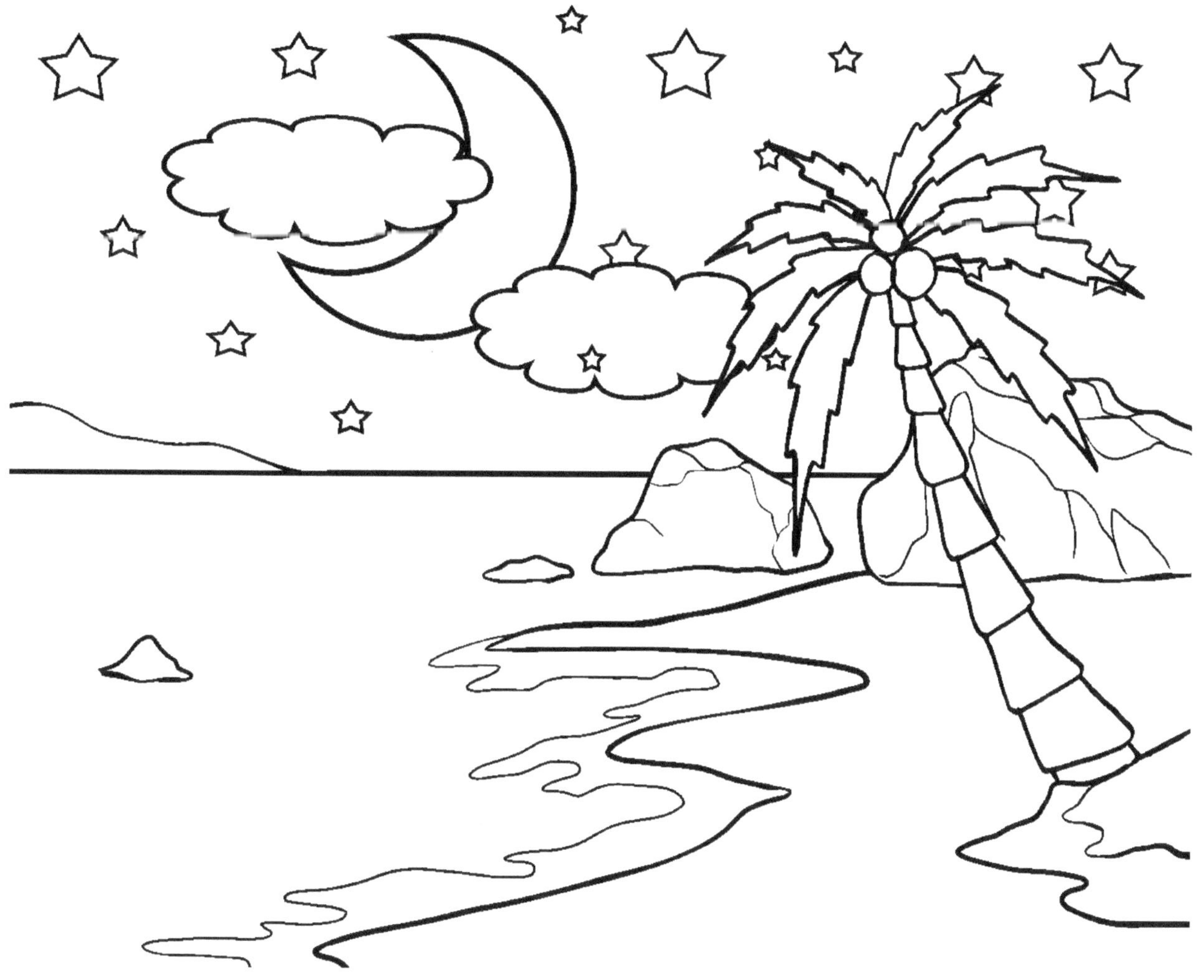

Nights and days came and passed and summer
And winter and the rain.
And it was good to be a little Island.
A part of the world and a world of its own
All surrounded by the bright blue sea.

~Margaret Wise Brown
The Little Island

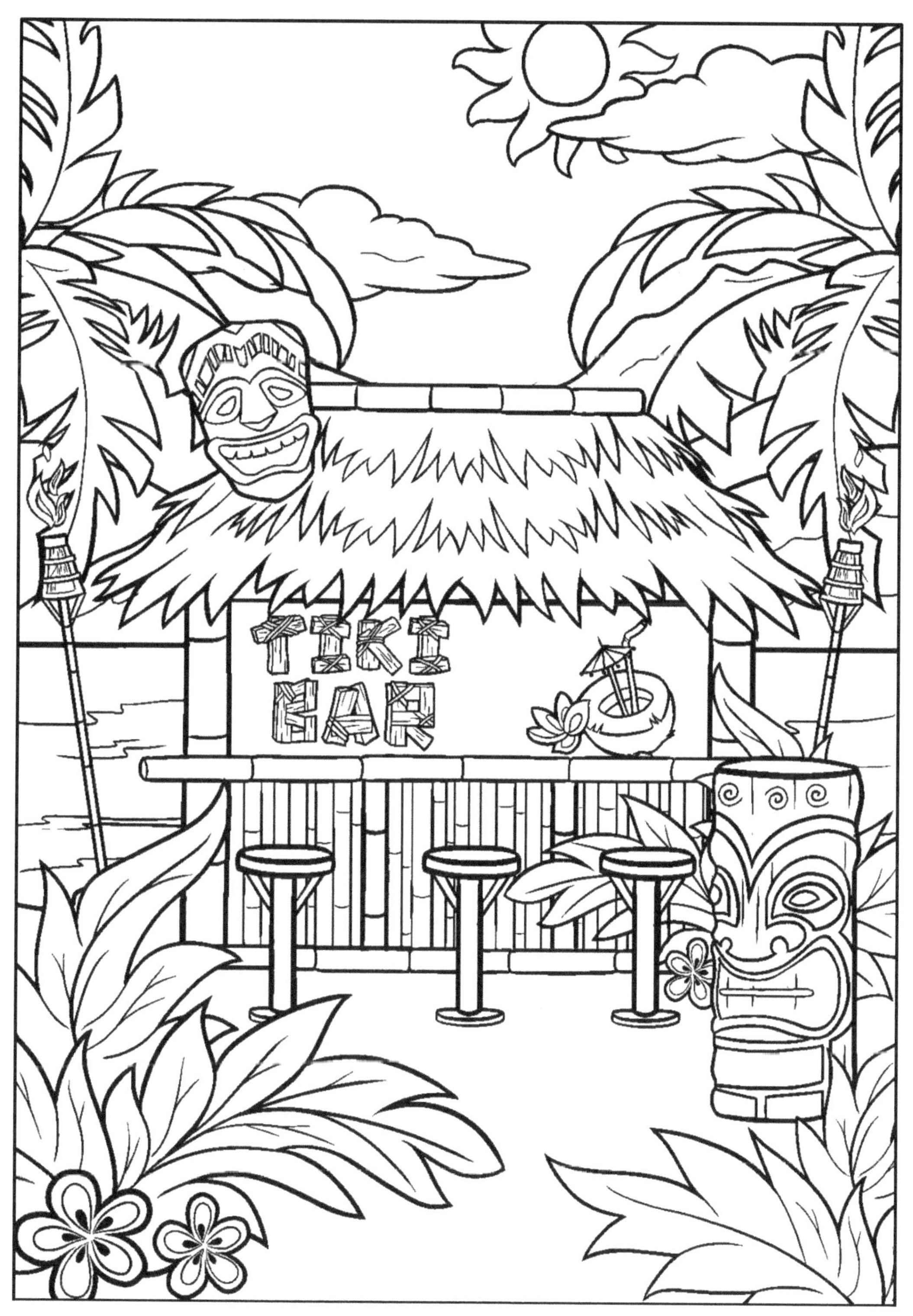

At the beach, every hour is **happy hour**!

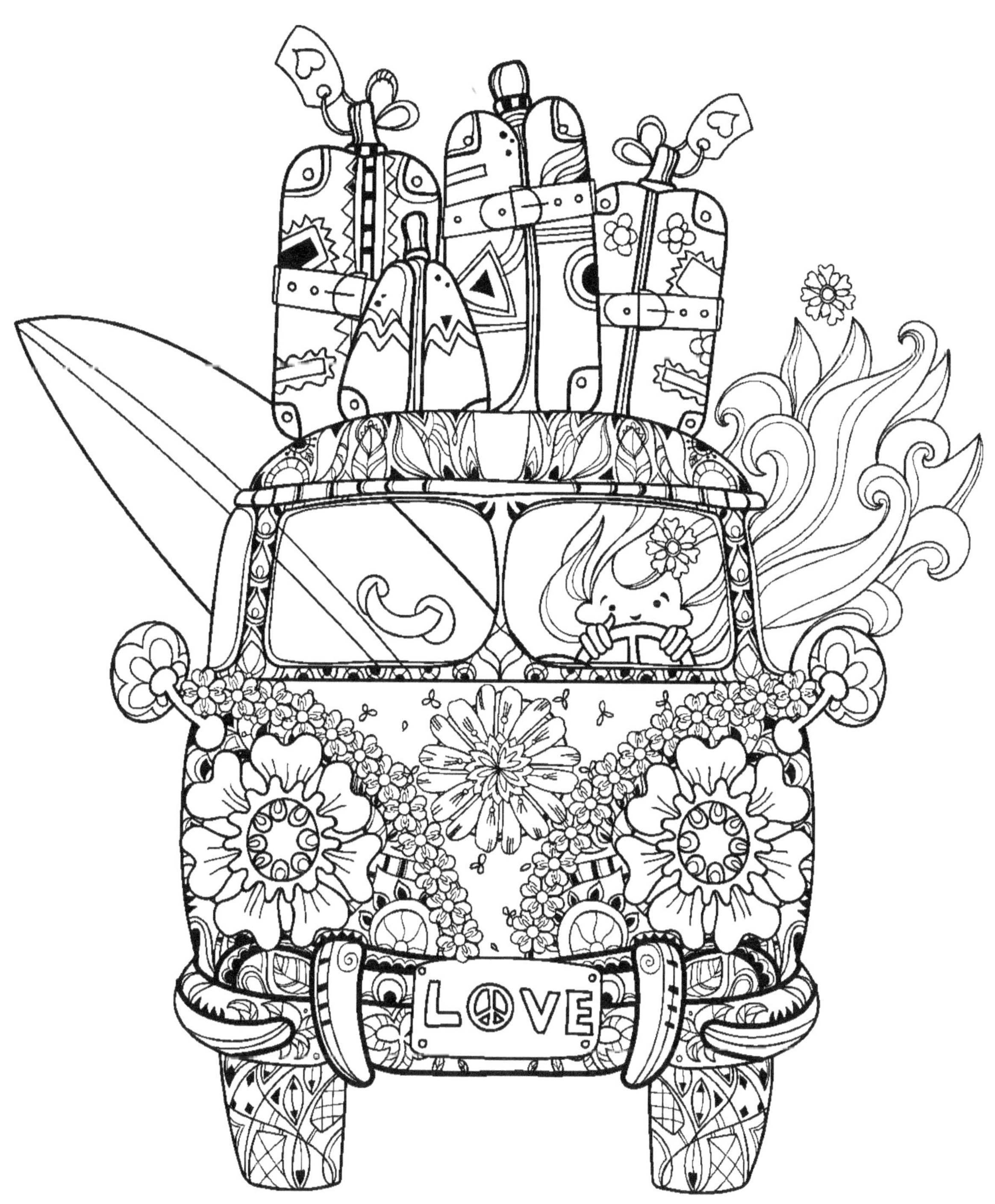

There is no cure for the travel bug so reserve a seat on your next journey! Until we meet again, I leave you with this: Of all the paths you may walk in life, make sure some of them leave your prints in the sand.

All My Best,
~Connie

Hi!

I hope you enjoyed traveling with me through ***Postcards From Paradise.***

Sign up for my newsletter and get free downloads, updates & private discounts when new books are released. Let's connect on social media, too. I'd love to hear from you!

AIR MAIL

Newsletter: www.conniegorrell.com

Facebook @ConnieSGorrell

Twitter @conniegorrell

Instragram @brentandconnie

I Wish You Happy & Safe Travels,

Connie

Thank you for your purchase of *Postcards From Paradise*!

Now let's have some fun!

1. Go on vacation. Soon. Tuck *Postcards From Paradise* into your beach bag. Okay, *staycation* if you must—we all need a break sometimes.

2. Take a selfie or photo of you using this book wherever you are. Show off your artistic flair on a finished masterpiece. Post it on social media, tag me and tell your friends to buy a copy for themselves, too!

Have a question?

Email our support staff: info@inspirations.international

The best things

IN LIFE ARE

the people we love,

the places we've been

&

THE MEMORIES WE'VE MADE

along the way

ABOUT THE AUTHOR

Tropic traveler, author, speaker, and mentor to many, ***Connie Gorrell*** has always been drawn to where the tropical trade winds blow, along with her husband Brent. Partial to the warm waters of the Caribbean, the couple has traveled from Hawaii to southern India and to remote, uninhabited islands in Central America during their travels.

Connie is a passionate advocate for women's well-being and education, inspiring women to become the best version of themselves. She has appeared on network and public television, radio, and international media. Connie is a featured writer for women's magazines, commercial magazines, newspapers, and online publications. She is the founder of the DreamSTRONG™ Foundation, a public charity designed to create prosperity through inspiration for women and girls via empowerment, enrichment, and education. "Anyone living life unfulfilled must find tools and inspiration to take control of their situation. I want to prove to every woman that she is entitled to live a rich and deserving life, and to exercise her God-given right to strive for her dreams—no matter what!" says Connie. "We must tell these stories."

Connect with Connie!

Website:	www.conniegorrell.com
Email:	connie@conniegorrell.com
Facebook:	@ConnieSGorrell
Twitter:	@ConnieGorrell
Instagram:	@brentandconnie

PUZZLE SOLUTIONS

#1. Easy Barefootin'

#2. Take the Long Way Home

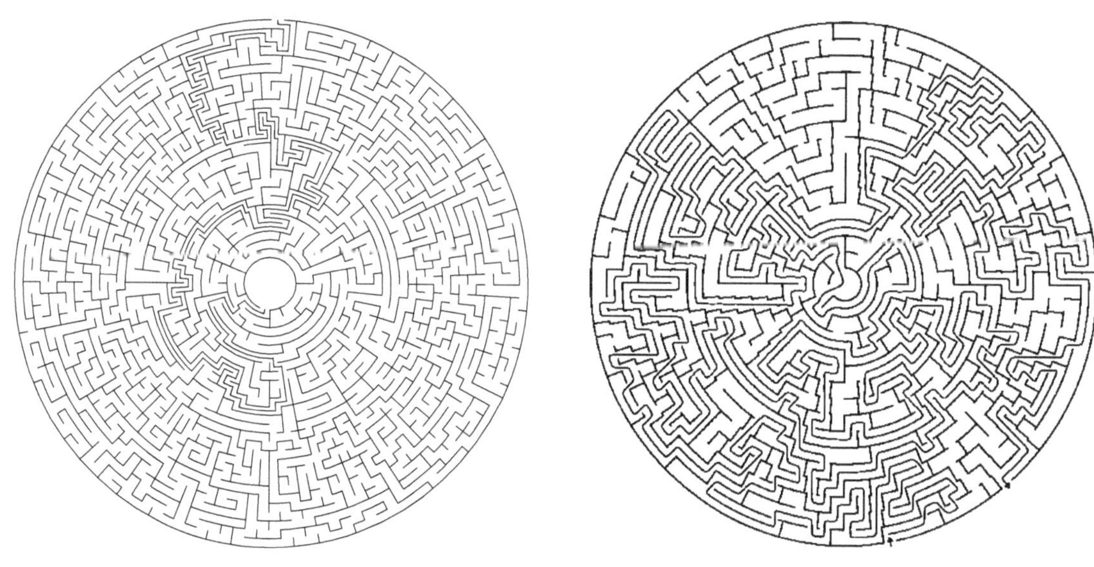

ISLAND FUN

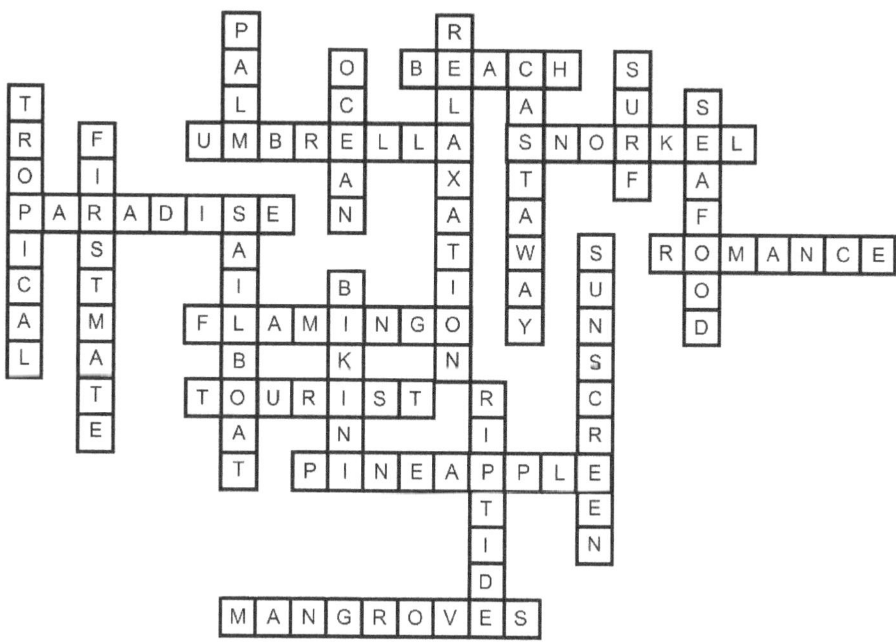

TROPICAL TROVE

```
D H B F M O I R E N S Y B I G C S U G H V E
K S P E Y H C K E L S A Y E M Q Q D S K X L
R I Q G A Z L R E R T W N K A U A K J C M S
A F Y T W C C B E Y U S A D N C N D U V U D
L R O A I P H I N S I S A G A I H R O N V E
L A Q V T J N B A I C E B C R L S T S F S G
O T Z M Y E G N A W R E L D D I S E O I A L
D S O Z V N A N U L Y R Y Q O N T E G W P X
D G T U G U O K I B L T F N H S A U C C E P
N T O K G I L G G C I M S G O G H S O C K L
A S C I A N P L R U N L W Y I K R R N U J C
S P E L I C A N R T J A L D G P A A C A F A
R A B I K I T F H J X P D A M L I T H L W B
E S I D A R A P M O R F S D R A C T S O P A
S U N T A N L O T I O N E E N L Q G H F M N
S E V A W N A E C O S N E N U A E I E O A A
S U N G L A S S E S E F A L A A C Y L L B B
S P O L F P I L F V A A K C Y L B I L N U O
S V J X X S L O Q M G I N B U P P D S X C Y
T B N Z F F V B H F U D D D N O V A L U S G
N H G S P R D X O L L I G X L I T I E T M Y
V D V K T U S Q W G L H K F K Q C B L S A O
```

THE SEAFARER

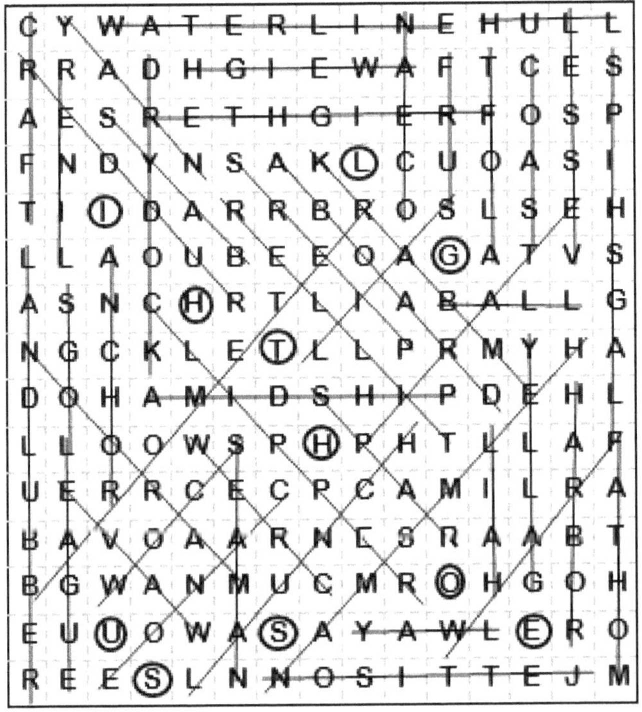

SECRET WORD: LIGHTHOUSES

SUDOKU:

EASY RIDER

5	4	3	7	1	8	9	6	2
6	1	8	9	2	3	4	5	7
2	9	7	4	5	6	1	3	8
1	6	2	3	9	7	8	4	5
3	8	4	5	6	1	2	7	9
9	7	5	2	8	4	3	1	6
4	3	9	6	7	2	5	8	1
8	5	6	1	4	9	7	2	3
7	2	1	8	3	5	6	9	4

TIPSY TOURIST

3	5	4	8	7	9	2	6	1
6	8	7	3	2	1	5	4	9
1	9	2	4	5	6	7	8	3
5	4	6	9	1	8	3	2	7
9	1	8	7	3	2	6	5	4
2	7	3	6	4	5	1	9	8
8	3	1	5	6	4	9	7	2
4	2	5	1	9	7	8	3	6
7	6	9	2	8	3	4	1	5

GALLOPING GLOBETROTTER

9	5	7	8	3	4	2	6	1
4	3	2	9	1	6	8	5	7
6	1	8	7	5	2	3	9	4
5	2	6	1	9	8	7	4	3
1	9	3	2	4	7	5	8	6
7	8	4	3	6	5	1	2	9
8	4	1	5	7	9	6	3	2
3	6	5	4	2	1	9	7	8
2	7	9	6	8	3	4	1	5

SEASONED JETSETTER

6	2	7	5	4	1	3	8	9
8	5	4	7	3	9	1	2	6
9	3	1	6	2	8	5	4	7
3	1	9	8	6	5	4	7	2
5	4	2	3	9	7	6	1	8
7	6	8	4	1	2	9	5	3
1	8	6	9	7	4	2	3	5
4	9	5	2	8	3	7	6	1
2	7	3	1	5	6	8	9	4

SENTENCE SCRAMBLER:

WE TRAVEL SO THAT WE CAN COME BACK; THEN WE SEE THE WORLD DIFFERENTLY. COMING BACK TO WHERE WE STARTED IS IN NO WAY THE SAME AS NEVER HAVING LEFT. OUR TRAVELS BECOME A PART OF WHO WE ARE.

www.ingramcontent.com/pod-product-compliance
Lightning Source LLC
LaVergne TN
LVHW081325110826
845149LV00007B/1599

9780998265124